T0371724

THE RIGHT CHOICE

Using Theory of Constraints for Effective Leadership

THE RIGHT CHOICE

Using Theory of Constraints for Effective Leadership

Ted Hutchin

CRC Press
Taylor & Francis Group
Boca Raton   London   New York

CRC Press is an imprint of the
Taylor & Francis Group, an **informa** business

A PRODUCTIVITY PRESS BOOK

MIX
Paper from
responsible sources
FSC
www.fsc.org **FSC® C014174**

CRC Press
Taylor & Francis Group
6000 Broken Sound Parkway NW, Suite 300
Boca Raton, FL 33487-2742

Library of Congress Cataloging-in-Publication Data

Hutchin, Ted.
  The right choice : using theory of constraints for effective leadership / Ted Hutchin.
     p. cm.
  Includes bibliographical references and index.
  ISBN 978-1-4398-8621-2 (hbk. : alk. paper)
     1. Theory of constraints (Management) 2. Leadership. 3. Decision making. 4. Organizational effectiveness. 5. Organizational behavior. I. Title.

HD69.T46H88 2012
658.4'092--dc23   2012013733

Visit the Taylor & Francis Web site at
http://www.taylorandfrancis.com

and the CRC Press Web site at
http://www.crcpress.com

For four very special people in my life and upon whom

the future depends—my grandchildren

Esme, Daniel, Fraser, and Isabel

Contents

Acknowledgments

I once wrote that we are each blessed by God with a wonderful range of gifts and that for some strange reason mine appears to the ability to observe, write, and teach, coach, and mentor in the world of leadership. What I find fascinating is that for a substantial period of my life I was not as aware of this gift, in the context of leadership, as others. I found it odd that people would ask me to coach them, mentor them, come to me for career advice, for guidance, and once I had offered my thoughts and walked with them for a while on their own particular journey of life, they would say farewell and offer thanks for all the help I had given them. It was only recently that it dawned on me that I was being led to do this and those who came to me did so because they felt that I would be able to help them, able to unblock them, able to open up their future when they felt all had been closed off. More recently, I felt a real sense of urgency to write down what I was doing, pulling it all together into some form of coherent approach, so that others might follow. When I suggested to colleagues and friends that I was thinking of this, the dominant response was one of surprise that I had not started many years before!

There have been many people who have helped me on this journey. Mentors such as John Garnett and Eli Goldratt, friends and colleagues such as Kathy Austin, Oded Cohen, Limor Winter-Kraemer, Danny Walsh, Tony Lumb, and many more who all helped me to seek both wisdom and understanding in what leadership is all about.

Thanks also to those who helped with the writing and the grind of checking for clarity, asking the awkward questions as to why I thought this way or that way, forcing me to challenge my own assumptions: Diane Jeary, Dave Stevens, and last but not least, Audrey, my wife, who always seems to find those aspects of my writing where clarity is missing with such verve!

Finally, to Alan Leader, a great man and an equally great friend who sadly passed away before this book was published and whose contribution to it cannot be underestimated. I will truly miss him. His friendship meant so much to me and also to the many people whose lives he touched. Thank you Alan, you will be long remembered and the moments we had together, discussing so many subjects, will be treasured forever.

Introduction

A BRIEF OVERVIEW OF LEADERSHIP

Over the years I have spent a great deal of time researching, writing, and coaching about the whole subject of leaders and leadership. I have come across so many wise and gifted people who have helped me greatly, and have unknowingly guided my own sense of direction for my life. I have read, and met, such luminaries as John Adair, John Garnett, Eli Goldratt, Meredith Belbin, Alistair Mant, Stephen Covey, and many more. I have sat and listened to what they had to say, challenged them, asked questions of them, and then tried to understand the answers! With my army background, I have sat in many lectures on the subject of leadership and taken part in exercises out in the field, both of which were designed to create within, or perhaps release from within me, some inherent, hidden leadership traits that might be able to express themselves on the battlefield. Thankfully, this was never put to the test during my time.

This book does not set out to review all the vast amount of material focusing on leadership that is available today, but it does try to explain some of the things I have witnessed over the years while working with leaders of all types in all manner of organizations, focusing on leadership at the three levels of personal leadership, team leadership, and organizational leadership.

In recent months, I have been able to visit a number of organizations of various types and sizes to look at the way in which they are led. At the same time, I have been fortunate to speak at various events on the subject of leadership and during those sessions, to determine just what the people attending thought leadership was all about. What has struck me about this is the level of importance given to the subject of leadership today. People seem to be very much aware of the importance of "management" but now recognize that in terms of "leadership" there is a real and present gap both in the knowledge of leading and also the execution of leadership. The number of people asking me for more information, books to read, courses

The Performance Gap?

- Regular and common problems
- Excess costs of delivery or non-delivery
- Lost sales and contracts
- Lost opportunities for sales or inability to open new markets
- Failure demand
- People fail to own direction or take responsibility for problems
- Low morale and unhelpful behaviors
- Poor management of performance
- Poor leadership of change
- Lack of skills
- Sense of not being in control

FIGURE I.1
The performance gap.

to attend—indeed anything to do with leadership—is on the increase, and in response to this ever-growing need for people who can actually lead I set out to write this book.

So from the time I started to think about this book, I took the opportunity to capture many of the statements about common issues and problems that people were making to me about the performance gap they thought existed, and these are listed in Figure I.1. Although this list came originally from manufacturing companies, I have also found the same issues appearing in nonmanufacturing companies, the public sector, the voluntary sector, and many other types of organizations, large and small. This led me to the conclusion that what I am discovering is much more universal than I previously thought.

At the same time, the pressure for a sense of direction has never been greater. This certainly applies at the level of the whole organization, but I have also found that it applies with the same force, and urgency, at the team level. The need for someone to say clearly and simply "this is the direction we need to take" has, equally, never been greater and yet so often is missing altogether. I came across many people who were managing the status quo with great skill and experience and yet said to me, at the same time, "I'm not sure if this is the right direction!" It was as if, in the absence of the real direction, any direction would do! There is often a clear recognition of the performance gap, and this is often matched with the

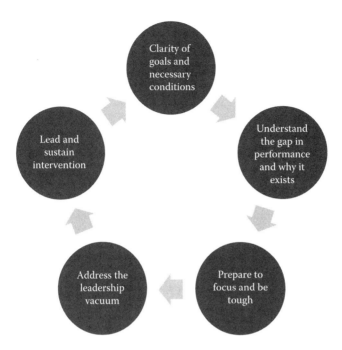

FIGURE I.2
The map of leadership.

similar recognition of a leadership gap. This leads of course to another observation which is, how do you know there is a performance gap when the direction is not clear? In most organizations I do find that there is a tacit understanding of the goal of the business, and even the necessary conditions (NCs) required to achieve the goal; what is missing is the clarity as to the goal/NCs and the strategy required to get there. This is, to my mind, one of the key characteristics of leaders, and thus one of their key contributions. They inspire people to journey toward the goal; they inspire people to see their true worth rather than simply as an expense item. They are able to communicate the goal, the direction, and to allow people to innovate, to create, to try different ways forward, unconstrained by artificial rules and procedures that stifle the very creativity most organizations need right now. This led to the development of a simple flow map of this, shown in Figure I.2.

Here I lay out the five steps that I have found good leaders are able to use in their engagement with the people within the organization. It starts as you might expect with the promotion of the goal and necessary conditions. This assumes they have been properly identified, developed, understood, agreed on, and finally, communicated. Then, using a measurement system that genuinely measures performance toward the goal, identify the performance gap and determine why that gap exists. This demands a measurement system that is holistic, therefore global, not focusing on the individual performance of the small entities within the system but always the system as a whole. The gap in performance only makes sense when it describes the global gap in performance for the organization as a whole.

The next step on the map is all about the importance of focus. Of course in our experience this is where the use of the Theory of Constraints Thinking Processes (TOC/TP) has huge impact and where much of our training/coaching support is applied. This is where the need to be both focused and tough really enters the equation. Leaders in this environment do not compromise on the pathway to the goal. They challenge the assumptions within the organization and at the same time the rules and procedures that currently exist, including measurement. If the existing rules and procedures help with the right behaviors, then they leave well enough alone; but if they do not, then leaders are not afraid to challenge them and change them if required. Focusing needs this dimension of toughness, the ability to maintain the focus even under fierce pressure not to do so. Being tough is about not compromising on the goal and a readiness to make the hard decisions.

It might seem odd to then suggest that the next stage on the map is to address the leadership vacuum, so a word of explanation. In the case studies that form the core of this book, many times I found the interesting fact that the overall leader of the organization was able to genuinely communicate what was needed, what the direction was going to be and so on—in other words, was able to demonstrate the level of understanding needed to be an effective leader. But once the baton had passed to those below this person, problems occurred. This is described in more detail later in Chapter 7 when I consider the impact that a conflict of worldview can have, leading to a conflict of paradigms. Leadership is not just the preserve of the person at the top, but it has to be seen, felt, given, and responded to throughout the whole of the organization. This leads to the inevitable conclusion that the role of leadership extends beyond the top person; it is for everyone to understand and communicate. It should also be noted that some of the case studies contained here were drawn from those who had people at the top who did not display any such confidence of leading their organization or team with any reasonable level of competence. This extended to the communication of whatever direction suited at that particular point in time.

Giving direction within an organization, or within a team, is a two-way activity and must be seen in that light. The case studies I have used demonstrate both those who were successful in this respect and those who were not. It shows the level of input necessary for such leadership to be effective, to be part of the life of the organization, focused and effective at all levels. The final stage of the map is creating an environment where this whole road map is understood and commonplace. This is where the organization becomes a learning organization, capable of sustaining the changes that are being implemented, capable of replicating what is being done in other areas as and when required, and of learning from the process, capturing key aspects, the hard points, the places of conflict and learning from them. This is an ongoing loop; once it has been completed the first time, then it is repeated again and again with others being brought into the leadership role throughout.

Although this book started out with the idea of looking at leadership in terms of either team or organization, or perhaps both, the reality quickly became clear that most of the people I was working with, and in some cases still work with, needed help in their own lives, whether it had to do with their work, or their family, or the community in which they lived. The importance of being able to make sound choices for themselves was as important, if not more so, than the choices they made at the team or the organizational level. Leadership is about making sound choices, choices of direction, toward something deemed to be of importance for the individual, the team, the organization, or combinations of all three. This then is the focal point of this book: developing the ability to make sound choices in life, choices that take me, or you, toward my or your goal in life. Choices that take my team toward the goal, take my organization toward the goal, these are the issues that I found so many people struggling with, and this book tries to tell their story, and how they set about doing something about this "leadership gap" using the Theory of Constraints (TOC).

Life as a Story

I am often amazed when working with new people, or joining a new group, at the stories the people tell of their journey to where they are now. This also applies to the details they seek from me about my own story. I hear from them the good and the bad, the highs and lows, the bits they are proud of, and the not-so-proud bits! I have sat and listened quietly as they have gone into great detail about the wonderful choices they have made, and the not-so-wonderful. There is a recognition here that "story" seems to define who we are and where we have come from. It also defines, I think, our current understanding about where we think we are going. All of these events, seen as a timeline, are part of this definition of who we are. We cannot change that which has happened in the past, no matter how much we might wish we could. Our past defines us. We are who we are because of our history. This is true whether it came about through our own choices or those forced upon us.

Therefore, we have come to this point in time as a result of all that has happened to date. Each person's story is unique and where we go from here depends on the choices we make now. Of course, some choices are ours to make, freely and without influence from any other source. Other choices are not so freely made, but they remain choices nevertheless. Even the statement "I have no choice" still contains an element of choice.

This book recognizes that my life, your life, is a story and one that has already contained a number of choice points: a point in our life when a choice was clearly before us and had to be made, for whatever reason. But how to make that choice and having made a choice, what then? But then there is the journey that follows the choice made. Did I arrive at the destination the choice suggested I would? Or was I faced with more decisions, each a direct function of the choice made? And were all these decisions easy for me to carry out, or were some more difficult than others? Did some of the decisions I had to make, or still need to make, give me cause for concern, or even an urgent desire not to make them? Perhaps I could see pain for someone, if not myself, if I made the decision? Perhaps I would prefer it if someone else made the decision that I considered to be so difficult?

There is a final group of decisions that I found to be problematic. They are those truly awkward decisions that seem to violate the whole idea of how I see myself; they seem to go right to the heart of who I think I am, and how others see me. There is no way I wish to make this decision; it is too painful by far. There is no way the actions that are contained within the decision will ever be done by me—this is truly a step too far. This is my sticking point. I may have gone along with everything else so far, but not this. I don't care if my decision not to execute the decision that is before me causes concern, or even harm, or even causes the team and/or the organization to not move forward, to stay where it is, perhaps even to close. I am choosing here to deny the choice I so readily made beforehand, before I understood the consequences of that first choice, for it so violates my own story that I cannot, and will not, do it. This, too, is part of the story of this book.

Then there is the wider perspective of my team and/or my organization. Was I able to bring them with me, lead them in the right direction? Was I able to encourage them to join me on the journey? How did it feel when it went well, and how did I feel when it did not? Was I frustrated that "they didn't get it" or I felt "why should I bother" and a host of other emotional responses!

Here is an example from my own life. In 1964 I was trying to determine a career for myself once I had finished school. I had a real interest in physics and, in particular, radar. Now I was offered two choices, and the first was to complete my schooling and take up an apprenticeship with Ferranti Radar which was located in my hometown of Edinburgh. The other choice was to take up an apprenticeship with the army, the Royal Electrical and Mechanical Engineers (REME). Both had positives and negatives, both opened up opportunities, and after weighing the two choices, seeking advice, and asking myself which I preferred, I decided to choose the REME. This then meant that a whole raft of decisions followed that choice. Had I chosen the civilian pathway, the decisions would have been different—not all of them, but enough. The choice of the REME also meant that decisions would appear throughout my career that I may not have foreseen at the start but were still part and parcel of the choice I had made. For most of my career in the army, I went along with the decisions I was asked to make, but eventually I started to have to make decisions that I did not want to comply with and the inevitable happened. I could no longer subordinate to those decisions and I left. So my story followed the sequence of choice followed by decision, followed by, over time, an inability to subordinate to those decisions. Some of my friends continued with their journey inside the army, but I felt compelled to leave and did so. Of course, leaving the army was also a choice, and that too followed the same sequence.

The Entry Point Called "Relationships"

The entry point to the story of this book is about the relationships we have with those around us. I have used a simple model throughout the book, one that discusses three aspects of our lives where relationships are fundamental to our sense of just who we are, and which contribute to our unique story. These are the world of work, the world of family, and the world of the community in which we live. This is a simplification, I know, but it seems to be a pretty common simplification and one that works for most of the people I work with. There is considerable overlap between these three. I have found that for some people one so dominates that the other two barely measure on any scale. I have met people who recognize and live with dysfunctional relationships, broken relationships, a sense of being lost or alone, making irrational decisions that quickly affect not just their personal life, but also the team and the organization in which they work. This does not just mean paid work; the same applies to those who work inside voluntary organizations where pay is not the dominant reason for being there.

The whole question of work–life balance has never been so critical. Recent research studies in the United Kingdom have highlighted the dramatic impact a lack of balance can bring to almost all relationships. In my work over the years, I sat with people who recognized this imbalance and at the same time had no idea how to address it. Part of why this book was written was to tell the story of these people, how they started with a voyage of discovery about who they really were. This process of "knowing yourself" is such a fundamental starting point, yet so many people feel afraid to embark on their journey from this point. It is recognized by many practitioners in coaching and mentoring that without this understanding about your "self" it is difficult to make any real progress in knowing others, and certainly in the dynamic of leadership.

In this book, I have set out to describe something of what is meant by "effective leadership." This is set in the context of the goal and the necessary conditions to achieve that goal. It is about striving to achieve excellence in everything we do. Smith and Shaw (2011) note, "Excellence is not just what we do but is an attitude. It comes from the way that we view our work and how we do it. Excellence attracts excellence, it inspires excellence" (p. 38). This statement certainly echoes much of my own belief in leadership and relationship building. We have to live what we believe, show that what we are proclaiming is how we ourselves believe life should be lived. Smith and Shaw continue, "Excellence originates from the leader. If the leader does not exemplify and practice it then standards will never be raised and people will be happy to put up with second best. Excellence has to be seen and experienced at every level and in every activity of the organisation" (p. 38). So, assuming this is agreed, let the journey begin.

REFERENCES AND FURTHER READING

Belbin, R. M. *The Coming Shape of Organisation*. Oxford, UK: Elsevier Butterworth Heinemann, 1996.

Belbin, R. M. *Beyond the Team*. Oxford, UK: Elsevier Butterworth Heinemann, 2004.

Belbin, R. M. *Management Teams: Why They Succeed or Fail*. (2nd Edition) Oxford, UK: Elsevier Butterworth Heinemann, 2004.

Covey, S. R. *The 7 Habits of Highly Effective People*. London: Simon & Schuster, 2004.

Garnett, J. *The Work Challenge*. London: The Industrial Society, 1973.

Goldratt, E. M. *It's Not Luck*. Aldershot, UK: Gower, 1995.

Goldratt, E. M. *The Choice*. Great Barrington, MA: North River Press, 2008.

Smith, A., and P. Shaw. *The Reflective Leader*. Norwich, UK: Canterbury Press, 2011.

1

Setting the Scene

BACKGROUND TO THE BOOK

I have been very fortunate over the years to have worked in some amazing organizations all around the world. My involvement in the Theory of Constraints (TOC) has opened doors to travel and working with people that I could never have imagined while teaching me a great deal about the issues and problems these same people have to struggle with each and every day. In almost all cases, those I met were really keen to see their organization improve. They had read books such as *The Goal* (Goldratt, 1984) and many others. They had seen the case studies from the various TOC conferences over the years and thought that such performance would be just what their company needed. They then came to the TOC programs that I was running and set out to put their organization onto a real process of ongoing improvement, one that was sustainable, scalable, and replicable. It had to be a process that they could do for themselves, so there had to be knowledge transfer—the skills and the techniques of the TOC approach had to be transferred into the organization for it to be truly successful.

The key questions that the program sets out to answer are as follows: What to change? What to change to? How to effect the change? And finally, how to maintain the change? So taking each one in turn, answering the question "what to change?" is focused on identifying the real blockage within the organization preventing it from moving forward toward the goal, that single entity that is the cause of most of the problems and issues facing the organization right now. This identification demands clear thinking, a robust process, and the ability to communicate both the analysis and the conclusions in such a way that all agree that this "thing" is the core problem and we must remove it. Answering the second question, that of what to change to, takes the answer to the first question and then, using the same logical structure, builds the solution, noting the key changes that are necessary to achieve the desired state. This is where we paint a compelling picture of what the future might look like and communicate the whole analysis once more in order to ensure that there is a wide consensus that this is the direction we have to follow. Making it happen starts with the implementation plan, how are we going to achieve the objectives, the changes, that are required for the solution to work, and then finally, how do we maintain the new state, maintain progress toward the goal from this new vantage point? After we have gone round this loop once, it is usual to do it all again, and again, and each time the level of performance is higher and the gains greater. We will return to this process later in the book.

Over the last five or six years, however, I noticed that for many organizations the work done was often leading people to question just where the organization was going. Then I found them questioning the direction of their team, and finally the direction of their own life. At this point, I changed tack when engaging with any new client, moving away from the traditional TOC approach of working with a client in production or project management, implementing well-proven approaches such as Drum Buffer Rope (DBR) and Critical Chain Project Management (CCPM) to, what was for me a radical departure, coach rather than train, to mentor rather than run courses.

What I had discovered lies at the heart of this book and has led me to see the whole area of leadership in a new light, working at the three levels of organization, team, and self. This went well beyond just manufacturing companies to organizations of all types and people at all levels. I found that this new approach worked in the service sector, the public sector, and the voluntary sector. I decided that I should go back to the research and related work I completed at the end of 1998 and use that as the starting point, the foundation, for this present work.

SOME HISTORY!

Between 1993 and 1997 I had spent a great deal of time examining the implementation of TOC throughout the United Kingdom, Europe, and the United States as part of my research at Cranfield University. The primary result of this work was the publication of my book *Unconstrained Organisations* in 2001. It is pertinent to revisit that study in the light of events since then, colored by what I have learned on my own journey of discovery about leadership within organizations. Then the focus of the research was to determine the barriers to change facing those seeking dramatic improvement to the bottom-line of their organization, and in that respect I was able to describe a primary barrier to change, which I called "paradigm lock" (see Chapter 7). What I set out to consider in the research for this book were some of the assumptions that formed part of the foundation of that original study and then to ask one simple question—just how effective were the leadership approaches being used at the time and has anything changed today?

Then, as now, I feel real pain when I see organizations closed when much more could have been done to keep them not only open, but growing. The years of working with the TOC approach have convinced me that the art, or maybe the science, of leadership is missing in many organizations. Couple this lack of leadership with the dominance of cost-based measurements used for making decisions, and the scene is set for real problems which lead, in turn, to real tragedy, closed companies, people out of work, communities suffering. Often I have pondered, is it necessary for so many to fail, for so many to appear in the obituary columns of the *Financial Times* or *The Wall Street Journal*?

As I started to write this book, I quickly became aware of a number of key factors in the leadership question. The first, and perhaps most dominant, was that today, many people seem unable to challenge dominant paradigms as to how businesses are run. This applies to all types, private, public, voluntary, large and small, and across all national boundaries. It would appear that the dominant worldview of how to run a business is set in tablets of stone with no opportunity to challenge the perceived wisdom of the age. This is certainly the case in the United Kingdom but perhaps not so prevalent elsewhere. This then leads to real questions about how to take an organization forward in the difficult times of today, how to lead organizations when the pressures are what they are today. The current pressure in the public sector in the United Kingdom has led to many organizations, such as the National Health Service (NHS), the fire service, and the police to examine just how to get more for less, deliver more services for less investment including people.

It is within the UK context that I soon recognized that the inability to challenge the dominant worldview was itself a prime factor in many organizations facing difficulties even when the way forward was known, at least in part. This raises in my mind the application of the paradigm lock idea to the capacity to lead. Indeed this often begs the question, can we lead, and do we have people capable of leading organizations? Of course the answer has to be yes, there are many successful organizations in the world today, so it can be done. But at the same time why do so many fail?

―――――――――

SO WHAT IS LEADERSHIP, AND WHAT DO I MEAN BY EFFECTIVE CHOICES?

Over the past twenty-one years, I have worked with many people, in all manner of organizations with all manner of problems and issues, to resolve those issues and help them move forward using the TOC approach. They have held senior positions and have had the requirement as part of their role to improve the performance of the organization they were responsible for.

It might be reasonable to think that they were all very different, thus allowing me the opportunity to use the full range of the Thinking Processes (TP) within the TOC to gain best advantage, but you would be wrong! It almost always came down to their ability to make effective choices—and this remains the same today. But what do I mean by "effective choices"?

Almost all of the people I worked with were trying to work their way out of problems and issues—some were personal, some were related to the team they were working in, some were related to the organization they were working in—and some were a combination of all three! But what it really boiled down to was this: "Can we make sound choices given the situation we are currently in?" To which the answer appeared to be "not really." This was part of their pain: They knew what had to be done, but the actions required came from such a different paradigm, one that so conflicted with the dominant paradigm, that this set of actions was not an option.

OK, SO WHY THE FOCUS ON MAKING CHOICES?

If you are faced with having to make a choice in your life, or your team, or your organization, or any combination of those, how are you going to do it? Of course, some people put off the time to make the choice. They say "come back when I have more control" or "I can't deal with what you have to offer right now; come back later."

There is a theme in those responses, which is that for most people who answer this way, by the time they actually asked me for help, it was too late, or at the very least the situation was much worse than when the first discussion took place.

SO WHY DO PEOPLE DELAY?

When I started to examine the aspect of delay in more detail I found the following:

1. People were afraid to make the choice, any choice; this fear can come from a variety of sources, from someone else in the team or organization, perhaps at home or in the community. It can come from inside the person, when the choice offers little or no respite from what is going on. In fact, I have found numerous sources of such fear. However, in general it is not the source of the fear that matters but the response to it that counts. It should also be noted that for many people the perception of fear is just as "real" as the reality itself.

2. They had no way of checking to see which is the "right" choice to make. This is as much about the inability to determine outcomes from either choice, or at least to determine any negative outcomes, as anything else. There is a kind of hope that "it will be all right on the night" about this aspect, as if the execution of whichever choice made will remove any possible negatives, often followed by "but what if it does go wrong?" But more often than not this was also about an inability to determine the choice in connection with the journey toward the goal, and the necessary conditions that must be satisfied for the goal to be achieved.

3. They had no idea what the consequences might be, and no way of trying to analyze those consequences. Many people trying to lead will first object to any critical assessment of the choices being considered and then, if constructive criticism is given, they have no means of assessing, validating, or proactively and systemically scrutinizing it. They rely simply on an emotional level of response rather than a logical one.

4. They might not be at risk if they did nothing, but if they did something, anything, and it went wrong, they would surely catch all of the blame. The blame culture in many organizations, teams, and even at home seems to pervade many relationships. Their thinking is along the lines of "It is far better to stay outside of the decision-making process than to try to lead it, that way I cannot be blamed for any negative that will surely happen, this way I can move up the organization, keep my place without fear," and so on.

5. And anyway, the crisis might go away....

This is a fascinating set of answers, though by no means comprehensive, and often betrayed real pain. The fear was real, the lack of clarity was real, the lack of any understanding of consequences was real, and there was always the fall-back position—don't make any rash decisions; simply wait for someone else to make a choice, any choice!

WHY DO WE HAVE TO MAKE CHOICES?

I introduced the existence of the performance gap in the introduction, and this is a core driver in the making of a choice. The recognition, at the level of the organization, that we are not moving toward the goal (assuming we have a goal) is often cited as a valid reason for having to make a choice. At the same time, our relationships are often broken, fractured, difficult, awkward, etc. We want to transform them, and this too requires a choice to be made—and there are many more reasons that are offered. This applies to us as individual people when we feel that our lives are not going in the direction we wish them to take, when the issues that affect us at home, or at work, or within our community become so problematic that we feel we have to do something. The same happens when we are members of a team, whether the leader or just one of the team. We have seen dysfunctional behaviors tear teams apart and create all manner of conflicts which remain unresolved often over considerable timescales; of course the organization does not escape the same. They too are constantly trying to reconcile conflicting demands, conflicting pressures, conflicting desires, hopes, and aspirations. So here we have two distinct needs, the need to make a choice, and the need to both give and respond to leadership.

WHAT IS A CHOICE?

It is a decision we have to make between two competing entities or options—at a minimum! In most cases, we are faced with a choice as a function of our goal and necessary conditions. This might apply to us as individuals, or as members of a team, or even for our organization. So if we look at Figure 1.1, in the D box we can write the first choice, and in the D' box the other choice.

The assumptions that keep them in conflict are, for example, the two choices are not capable of coexistence at the same point in time, or they cannot both be done even at different times. There are obviously more assumptions that could be raised, but that is enough for now. The issues move to the simple answering of the question, given the problem(s) I am faced with, how do I make a good choice between two competing approaches both of which are valid and provide a solution to the problem as it has been defined? Whatever the context the same problem exists—"how do I make a good choice?" and what is a "good" choice anyway?

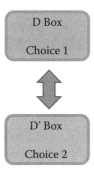

FIGURE 1.1
Simple choice conflict.

A WORKING DEFINITION

For me a "good" choice is one that at least meets some of the following:

1. Moves me toward my goal in life
2. Moves my team toward the team goal
3. Moves my organization toward the global goal
4. Does not negate any necessary conditions for the achievement of all the above
5. Transforms all my relationships to win-win
6. Has no significant negative consequences that I can't deal with

However, change implies choices, and choices imply change! Many senior people within organizations today are faced with having to make choices between competing options for direction toward the goal, and having chosen, they are then faced with a set of decisions related to that choice which leads to an important discovery for some people: *Changing the choice, changes the decisions.* Having made the choice they then find that not everyone is keen to implement the decisions mandated by the choice. This means that some people find it very difficult to subordinate to the decisions even if they were involved in the original choice process! Therefore, the demand for change forces choices, which in turn are subject to constraints. This typically results in the organization being blocked; it also results in the team being blocked—and finally the individual also finds himself, or herself, blocked as well!

SO HERE WE ARE!

Stay as we are or risk the change is a choice, and then, what are the implications of staying as we are? What are the implications of changing? In both choices, there are pros and cons—so how to choose? This assumes we know what to change to—so what happens if we don't? For an organization, this is often all about the conflict between growth and stability—we all want growth, but not at the expense of stability—but how to achieve both? So what can be said at this point? There can be no doubt as to the existence of numerous conflicts when it comes to making a choice. The range of options ranges from two to many. As a simple example, try asking for a coffee in Starbucks and see what happens—and remember all you wanted was a simple cup of coffee!

Common Issues

- Life is difficult
- There are daily conflicts
- My priorities are constantly changing
- My frustration is high
- My life is out of balance both at work and at home
- High levels of health-related problems
- Home life is affecting my work life and vice versa
- Things may be tough but at least they are known, better the devil I know than the one I don't
- Sense of not being in control

FIGURE 1.2
Common issues for the person.

WHAT IT MEANS TO BE BLOCKED— THE INDIVIDUAL LEVEL

At the level of the individual person, we have often captured the issues shown in Figure 1.2. This is not the most comprehensive list ever collected, but over time the issues raised here are the most common—indeed they are all too common.

They affect the people concerned in a variety of ways, both in terms of health, sense of well-being, and of feeling valued. Often I have been told that if only work could be easier, if only I could take a short break, if only I could feel at peace, even for a short while, if only…and so it goes on. Unblocking the individual remains the most challenging and yet the most rewarding part of my own work, and the process will be discussed in much more depth in Chapter 6.

WHAT IT MEANS TO BE BLOCKED—THE TEAM LEVEL

While working with an individual person is the most challenging, the most common area to try and unblock people is at the level of the team. Some years ago I worked with a group of forensic scientists and used the combination of the Theory of Constraints Thinking Process (TOC/TP) approach and the

Belbin Team Analysis methodology to help them develop a new, and better, way of working. It proved to be a very informative exercise as the combination of the classical team roles identified by Belbin and the issues addressed through the use of the TP tools allowed me to not just address some of the core issues but also to recognize the links between the team roles and the types of conflicts and issues that the team as a whole needed to address. The fact that they were not functioning as they should was not in question, but to see the understanding that grew as they recognized that unblocking was not a simple task and required a great deal of effort to solve was illuminating. The level of dysfunctional behaviors was high, there was a lack of focus across the whole of the organization, some took umbrage from comments that others saw as merely a statement of the obvious, and the potential for destructive behaviors was high. This was not an isolated example, as I have come across much such behavior in team environments. My time as both a rugby coach and sailing coach highlighted not only the need for brutal honesty between team members, but also a ruthless understanding of the commitment to achieve the goal. Technique was a given; it was mindset that made, and still makes, the difference. I have seen teams with high skill levels beaten by a team of lower skill but far greater cohesion and commitment to each other and the goal. When working in any type of organization, and in particular the caring professions, seeing these levels of dysfunctional behavior, the endemic blame culture, the current, dominant focus on trying to meet a whole raft of measures, many of which conflict, rather than the goal; is heartbreaking and at the same time often condemns the team to failure.

So I find many teams that are blocked from making progress, especially in terms of the relationships within the team and to those outside, and the list tends to include the issues already cited in Figure 1.2 plus a few more, such as: conflicts abound; projects I am associated with fail; ideas get dropped or stolen; rules and procedures are not followed; other people think they know better; there are simply too many obstacles standing in the way of our progress. This litany of problems and issues is, once more, commonplace.

WHAT IT MEANS TO BE BLOCKED— THE ORGANIZATIONAL LEVEL

And is it any different across the organization as a whole? No. Over the years I have come across too many organizations that are blocked from making progress; blocked in terms of performance measured by the bottom-line measurements; blocked in terms of the market; blocked in terms of change; blocked in terms of developing people to lead; indeed blocked in all manner of ways. All this combines at the team level right down to that of the individual to create an atmosphere of distrust, or holding back information, of protecting my back or that of the team, keeping my head down in order to avoid the "consequences" that must follow the lack of progress toward the goal. The issues I have described at the level of the individual and the team feed into the situation at the level of the whole organization and vice versa. It is painful to see people trying desperately to take the organization forward only to be thwarted at almost every step because of the paralyzing fear of failure and the almost complete lack of leadership throughout the whole of the organization. Couple this with the realization that those trying to lead are often undermined by those you might expect to share that leadership role and the picture is even more depressing. But it need not be like this. This scenario is not written in tablets of stone; it can be changed.

The aim of this book is to try to help people move forward in their life using the TOC/TP approach. By applying the tools and techniques described here in such a way that the potential that resides in every organization, in every team, and within each person is released.

Of course, as already noted this is all about direction—knowing the goal and the necessary conditions—and the need to make changes (choices) that take us toward that goal. It is about helping them to break free from where they are stuck, in any context. It is about helping them make informed choices, ones that lead toward the goal, and using the TOC/TP to do so…why? *Because I, and many others, have found it works.*

SOME ASSUMPTIONS OF MY OWN

When I started to write this book I knew that I had to set some limits, a boundary outside of which I was not going to stray; at least that was the hope. The data I collected as the case studies were all from the world of work, but I think it important to at least give some indication of where the primary case studies come from.

Some are from companies active in some form of manufacturing, whether it be the manufacture of new product or the "maintain and repair" activities necessary to keep a product, such as an aircraft, going. Two of these companies are rather large, and others are rather small. Indeed one of the most interesting examples is a small manufacturing company that was already growing when I started, and has continued to grow. I say that, as many of the larger companies that form the research data were not as effective as this example. Other organizations that are featured include the Health Service in the United Kingdom, the Anglican Church also in the United Kingdom, and other companies from both the service and voluntary sectors. I wanted to have a wide range of companies and organizations in order to check the validity of my assumptions and also to see if the ideas I was trying to validate were capable of transfer from one type of organization to another. I also sent out a rather simple little research questionnaire to many of the TOC practitioners I know around the world, including those who teach TOC and those who use TOC within their own companies. I invited them to think about the Thinking Process (TP) toolset, which ones they used the most, which ones they did not use and why, and which in combination. How did the tool(s) used help them in their own leadership role; how did it help them unblock themselves, their team, and their organization; and what lessons did they gain, indeed did they change the use of the tool to make it more effective? I chose these people primarily because they are my peers and their experience will either confirm my own or challenge it, which is exactly what I expect from them. But I also chose them because they have, cumulatively, much more knowledge and experience than I can ever hope to have, and that is knowledge that should be shared. The case studies and the responses from my research capture exercise will be covered later in the book (see Chapter 2).

The second basic assumption was to examine the impact on three distinct aspects of people's lives: impact at home, impact at work, and impact within the community (see Figure 1.3).

I know the diagram in Figure 1.3 is a simplification, and that our lives are much more complex than three circles with the three focal points chosen. But it seemed to work. The people involved in the case studies confirmed that it is these three areas of their lives that dominate, and the outcomes were of sufficient importance for me to go with it. What will become clearer as we travel through this book is that the place of most interest is the little part in the middle where the three circles overlap; that is the bit of us that impacts all the other areas of our life, the place that drives all our relationships. There is another aspect to the diagram in that over time I have gradually come to recognizes, which is that although I have drawn the three circles the same size,

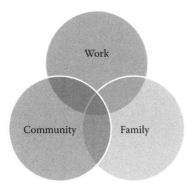

FIGURE 1.3
The three areas of focus.

in fact, this often is not the case. The balance between these three aspects of a person's life is not always the same as the diagram suggests, and when I have asked people to draw the three circles for themselves one usually dominates, one is smaller, and one may barely register! In many cases the "work" circle is the one that dominates, often many times bigger than the other two. I have then found that the third circle, "community," might cover a range of things, such as golf or some other external activity that the person uses in order to vent the passion raised at the dominant one—usually work! This leaves the final circle, that of family or home, and what I discover here is that this aspect is often placed third, and a distant third at that. Thus the impact of the dominant circle is to push the other two into a subservient relationship with all that entails. Therefore, in terms of relationships I have found many who are in a leadership role who "chose" to give most time and energy to where that role was being played out, recognizing the trade-off with the other aspects of their life. Many would say to me that the "work-life balance" was wrong and that they knew they had to "do something"! "But what?" they would ask me; they had made a choice. They followed their career and the responsibilities that went with that, but they then found themselves locked into a place they did not want to be and saw no way out.

The third aspect of the data capture was to confirm something I had noticed for a while, that there is a hierarchy that starts with making a choice. I had started to examine this in my work during the 1990s but really didn't see the importance of it at the time, especially with respect to leadership. However, over the past ten years I have found I cannot escape the importance this seems to have. Via this book I hope to show just how to break free from the paralyzing grip the choice hierarchy creates for many people.

CHOICE HIERARCHY

The choice hierarchy starts with making a choice. How the choice has been made will be discussed later, suffice for this moment that a choice has been required, the analysis done, and the solution developed in such a way that a choice can be made. So the starting point for this is the fact that a choice has been made by whatever process is used today.

The flow within the hierarchy is as shown in Figure 1.4 and is critical to recognize and understand. Once we understand the importance of the choice, we are faced with the need to make decisions. In most cases, we make those decisions, carry out the actions that follow, and move on. However, often there are decisions that are not so simple, in which we find ourselves asking if we implement the decision what will the real consequences be? This then takes us to the place which I have called "conflict of subordination" and is where the importance of the decision and the need to carry it out comes a distant second to the impact, perceived or otherwise, that I can see will affect me if I do carry out the decision. The important aspect to recognize here is that although I fully agree with the choice, fully understand why this particular choice is by far the right way forward for the organization and the team, and for the most part every decision is one that I fully support and am looking

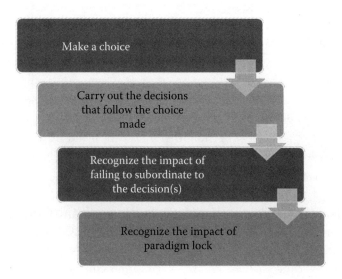

FIGURE 1.4
The choice hierarchy.

forward to seeing implemented, nevertheless this one decision is a step too far. I cannot make the actions this decision implies; in other words I fail to subordinate to the need for the decision to be implemented, and I refuse to carry it out.

AREA KNOWN AS "CONFLICT OF SUBORDINATION"

For the understanding discussed here, I am grateful to Suzie Hand who, as part of her MBA research project (Hand, 2001), carried out seminal work on this conflict and made some important observations. The critical nature of her research was not recognized for some time but now demands a much more in-depth assessment. She picked up this aspect of the hierarchy and set out to capture the data that confirmed the existence of this conflict and to consider how it might be addressed. Hand is herself a TOC expert in this field and had access to a variety of people in a number of organizations in a coaching role. She used the TOC/TP approach, which will be described in more detail in Chapter 3, entitled the "3-UDE Cloud," to analyze the issues. For more on this approach, see Scheinkopf's 1999 book *Thinking for a Change.* Suffice it to say at this point that the basic structure of a "cloud" comprises the five boxes shown Figure 1.5 and labeled A, B, C, D, and D'.

Figure 1.5 is used to articulate a conflict, and in the case of Hand's research, this cloud represents much iteration drawn from her data. The story this cloud diagram contains is as follows.

In order to *(be successful) achieve the objectives set for me (by myself and the organization)* **I must** *function as part of a team structure* **because**: *I cannot do it (the tasks) alone; the company is not just one person (me); this gains (me) respect from the other team members; this leads to satisfaction in my role with the team; and finally, teams achieve more than individuals.* The words after "because" are the assumptions that hold the two statements in the A and C boxes together. These assumptions, individually and collectively, are deemed necessary to hold the logic together. *We can now move to the next statement;* **in order to** *function as part of a team structure* **I must** *subordinate to the prioritization set by others* **because**: *this is the best process for achieving results; teamwork produces good results; and this is the most effective way to operate.* **However, in order to** *(be successful)*

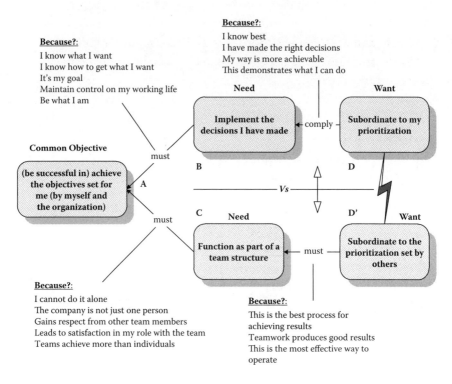

FIGURE 1.5
Conflict of subordination cloud.

achieve the objectives set for me (by myself and the organization) **I must** *implement the decisions I have made* **because***: I know what I want; I know how to get what I want; it's my goal; (I must) maintain control over my life, be what/who I am.* **And in order to** *implement the decisions I have made* **I must** *subordinate to my prioritization* **because***: I know best; I have made the right decisions; my way is more achievable; and this demonstrates what I can do. Finally, subordinate to my prioritization is* **in conflict with** *the prioritization set by others* **because***: the two are different; the two cannot be done at the same time; and that set by others includes those I report to.*

So the conflict captured by Hand is clear: The person caught in this conflict cannot achieve both the statement in D at the same time as that in the D' box. At the same time, if the person insists on carrying out the actions that are in line with his/her own prioritization (the D box), then the rest of the team do not see her/him as being a part of the team (the C box); and if the person complies with the prioritization set by others (the D' box), then he/she cannot, or at least perceives he/she cannot, implement the decision he/she has made (the B box).

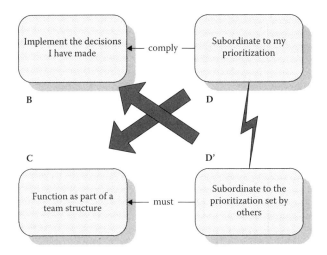

FIGURE 1.6
The cross-connection of the cloud.

This is known as "cross-connection," where what is written in the D box violates or jeopardizes the existence of the statement in the C box, and the statement written in the D' box violates, or jeopardizes, the statement in the B box (see Figure 1.6). In the case study developed by Hand, this conflict was commonplace and led to dysfunctional behaviors and broken relationships within the teams affected.

The final aspect of the choice hierarchy is where we meet what I defined as "paradigm lock" in my earlier work. I am going to develop this aspect of the hierarchy later in Chapter 7, so now we are ready to continue with the analytical process and consider the application of the TOC/TP tools in answering the question: what to change?

REFERENCES AND FURTHER READING

Goldratt, E. M. *Critical Chain*. Barrington, MA: North River Press, 1997.
Goldratt, E. M., and J. Cox. *The Goal,* 3rd ed. Aldershot, UK: Gower, 2002.
Hand, S. C. "An Analysis of the Barrier to Change Entitled 'Conflict of Subordination'" (MBA thesis, University of Leicester, UK, 2001).
Hutchin, T. *Unconstrained Organisations*. London: Thomas Telford, 2001.
Hutchin, T. *Constraint Management in Manufacturing*. London: Taylor & Francis, 2002.
Leach, L. P., and S. P. Leach. *Lean Project Leadership*. Boise, ID: Advanced Projects Inc., 2010.
Scheinkopf, L. *Thinking for a Change*. Boca Raton, FL: St. Lucie Press, 1999.
Schragenheim, E., and H. W. Dettmer. *Manufacturing at Warp Speed*. Boca Raton, FL: St. Lucie Press, 2001.

2

Some Thoughts on Leadership

WHAT DO I MEAN BY THE TERM "LEADERSHIP"?

I am well aware of the many books written on the subject of leadership, and it is not my intention to re-cover that ground here. But having started to explore leadership and what it means to me, I do think it helps to have some idea of what I think leadership is about. Of course, with an army background my whole view of leadership was conditioned by that training and experience. I met a few officers whom I felt the need to follow, some-times out of curiosity, sometimes because they inspired such a response, and the rest because they told me to! The same happened when I left the army and started to work in industry; some thought I would follow because they told me to and others were able to inspire me to do so. I have to say that the percentage split was not the way it should be or at least not the way I think it should be, but it was in line with what most people would recog-nize and experience today. "Do as you are told" seems to be a dominant way to lead! I have also come across many senior people today who lead by inviting everyone to vote on what should happen and are then surprised when there is paralysis because of a lack of direction being given by the top person. I have met many people who can manage, but noting all that has been said above, few who can lead, truly lead, truly inspire, truly capture the imagination and commitment of the people within the organization.

At a conference I attended in September 2007 entitled ProjectWorld, the main speaker was Stephen Covey. He used a term that I felt encapsu-lated what leadership, and indeed life, is all about. He stressed that "We must live life in crescendo," which said it all for me. Life is not for sitting back and waiting. The best is yet to come, he continued, and as I listened I went through all the many people I have met in all manner of organizations and asked myself a simple question, "How many are living life in crescendo?" and the answer was "not many." John Garnett, former head of the Industrial Society and one of my early mentors, gave the same advice to me when I left the army. For both men, it was about a sense of personal greatness and understanding that leadership is not a formal position in an organization, but it is primarily a choice centered on moral authority.

As I began to research this book, I found more and more that those who understood this aspect of leadership also understood the term "greatness" in a different way. It was not about seeking to have people honor you, but about developing the ability to inspire greatness in others, allowing them to achieve, even to have all the credit, about clarifying purpose and aligning the systems of the organization in such a way that talent was released, that intuition was given its head, and that by the careful use of questions and validating the answers people could and would reveal all manner of ideas and knowledge that hitherto remained hidden and dormant. This takes the concept of greatness to a deeper understanding of the creation of sustained superior performance at all levels coupled with the discipline of execution. Garnett, in particular, reinforced my understanding of, and the importance of, communicating worth to people so clearly that they are inspired to find it for themselves, and for the members of their team.

At the conference, Covey echoed the thoughts of many others when he argued that there are four elements of greatness, the first being the achievement of sustained superior performance compared to others in the same marketplace. The second concerned developing and maintaining an environment within the organization in which people felt they were "unleashed," able to really strive for excellence, and encourage the same for their own team members, knowing that all such effort took the team, the organization, and the people, toward their goal. Third, and this especially for those organizations with clients, such an approach will meet with a highly positive response from the customer base; they will want to work with such a company, and they will tell others about their experience, thus having a positive impact on the global market without any real activity from the company itself. The fourth and final aspect is that of understanding and encouraging the contribution of each member of the organization: a unique contribution that only that person could do, to make them feel truly valued, truly part of the team, and not simply an expense item to be dispensed with when times are hard.

Leadership starts, in my mind, with me. By that I mean that when I am in a position in which leadership is to be expected, then I should give it without question. It also means that, again as far as I can see, the way in which I lead is heavily conditioned by my own sense of personal greatness, the values and mindset I bring to the organization and the people, and my own values and sense of mission for the organization and all the people involved. I have always believed that leadership greatness is made up from a number of key ingredients, including being inspirational, demonstrating an ability to lead and enable others within the team and beyond to lead, and encouraging people to extend to levels of performance only dreamed of before. This means making sound choices, understanding consequences, ensuring discipline in the execution of tasks and roles, and living throughout all this with an exceptionally high level of personal integrity and compassion. It is my view that those who can achieve this find that such a way of working adds value to each person and to the bottom-line of the company.

In the execution of tasks, or changes, leaders make them happen. They focus, all the time, on the most important things as defined by the goal and the necessary conditions of the whole organization and leave the rest alone. They know the key metrics, those lead measures that everyone else should also be watching but are often not, and do this without sacrificing that which they are supposed to lead. These are always the measures that determine progress toward the goal and the achievement of the necessary conditions prescribed by the goal. Too many people manage only by maximizing their performance with respect to the local measures that apply to them and their area of responsibility.

However, leaders act only on the lead measures, and they understand that standing still is not an option and neither is prevarication; if action is needed they take the action, they make the choices that others wait for, they make the decisions that many shirk from, they lead, in other words. But they do not do so by being despots, by making all the decisions themselves. They instead create accountability throughout the organization; they devolve the key decision making to those below them, those that report to them.

Leaders are not afraid, or overly concerned, if someone should make a poor choice, a poor decision, for it is through such events that learning takes place. But leaders also ensure that no one is hurt by such an action, they take steps to ensure that when a choice is being made, when decisions are being made, there is a line of consistency throughout the whole of the organization in such a way that alignment of decision leads to alignment of purpose and progress toward the goal. Good leaders see themselves as the servants of those throughout the organization. It is their role to enable others to make the right decisions, to make things happen, to take the organization forward, to learn from mistakes; and this role extends into the future so that those that come behind are able to sustain progress toward the goal without thinking about the leader who has left.

This last takes us to the idea of what it means to leave a legacy. In a way this starts with understanding the needs of the people within the organization. What does the organization itself need, as a body of people, as a combination of a group of focused teams? What does the organization need in order to develop, to learn, to build up a body of knowledge and experience that those who follow can see and build on themselves? The effective leader sets out to answer these questions and to communicate the answers to all within the organization. There is an additional aspect to all this and that is the way in which people within the organization relate to each other. I have found that those organizations that truly excel are those that have a heart, those that encourage sound relationships, that dispense with the dominant paradigm of confrontation that seems to be the way most people see their role as either leader or manager, and replace that paradigm with one that seeks win-win resolution of all the conflicts and issues that arise. This is when I have seen a further aspect, that of creating a spirit within the organization that seeks to achieve, not by forcing but by encouraging, by engaging, by nurturing, by painting a compelling picture of what it could be like if we work as one and not as competing functions and teams.

Unfortunately I have found the prevalence of competing functions and teams to be commonplace in almost all the organizations I have worked with over the years. The culprit is the measurement system that sets up one against the other, that tries to ignore the reality of interdependence that is the true way with any system. This use of measures that assume independence between functions thus creates a fatal flaw within the organization, one that only leads to pain and often dramatic failure. This is hardly the legacy that most leaders would want to be remembered for!

Therefore, in this respect, I am advocating that leaders develop the ability to create a legacy which is formed by the principles by which the leader leads and lives. I have found that living by a clear set of principles, demonstrating consistent integrity in all aspects of life, remaining loyal to these principles, to their team, and their organization and true to that chosen way of life, is all part of what a leader is. I am often asked, by those I have been privileged to coach and mentor over the years, this question, "What are the individual, personal legacies that I might leave when I retire?" Often this is not an easy question to answer as the person asking it has shown no inclination to have any legacy at all, other than just be someone most people in the organization are keen to see the back of—which is hardly a legacy of note! But the question itself is critically important; many people I work with are keen to leave a legacy when they move on or retire, but often have no idea what it might be. I typically respond by asking the question back to them by inviting them to tell me what sort of legacy they have in mind. Is it one for themselves, for their team, or for the whole organization? Do they want to encourage others to be part of this legacy? I usually try to determine just what is driving the person, what lights the fire within their heart, what is their passion, what do they truly want to see achieved? It is in the answers to these probing questions that comments are made: comments alluding to the current poor performance however measured; the failure to take advantage of new opportunities whether it is in new markets or existing ones, in a new strategy, or simply getting on with the current one.

Often, there is recognition that the current system is not able to address some of these opportunities or issues, that there is no enthusiasm to change the current system, or that the person is not allowed to change it. I am told that the existing structures are not set up for meeting the new demand, a rising demand for which the systems required are not in place. Systems to deal with the new load that is being generated are often missing, and the skill levels of the people currently within the organization are not up to the required standard, or indeed, are missing altogether. What I find here is that many leaders within organizations are frustrated at their inability to lead change throughout the whole of the organization; they are struggling with teams who feel unable to carry through the changes necessary and with individuals who feel unable to participate in the change process, engage with it, contribute to it, and so on; and it is here that we can really start our journey. I have found some people state that they just seemed to be in the right place at the right time, and indeed we can be fortuitous in where we find ourselves and the people we have at our disposal, and sometimes we feel that luck has played a great hand. However, I should note at this point that many who feel they were placed in such a position often find that rather quickly luck runs out. Not for nothing did Goldratt write a 1995 book entitled *It's Not Luck*!

There is one last thought, at least for the moment, about leadership that is worthy of consideration at this stage. As far as I can determine, all the great leaders, whether it be in politics or the military, the church or industry, or any other facet of life today, have this in common: They inspire hope. Hope is an oft-misused word. Sometimes it is used in the offering of a future when, to all concerned, none appears to exist and at other times for opening up a future when everyone else thought such a future lost. Hope brings with it courage, an ability to overcome fearsome odds, to emerge victorious when all seemed lost. Hope brings endurance, to see difficult times through, for those within the team to gain strength from the clarity of purpose a leader brings at such a time. Hope also brings discernment, that fascinating, unique, ability to "know" that the direction is the right one, that the decisions that must be made are the right ones and however difficult they may be, they are part and parcel of achieving the goal and seeing all the hopes and aspirations gained.

THE STARTING POINT: THE TOOLS OF THE TOC THINKING PROCESSES

I have already stated that my way of coaching people as leaders is primarily through the use of the Theory of Constraints Thinking Process (TOC/TP). I was first introduced to this unique approach over twenty years ago by Eli Goldratt and Oded Cohen. The process was then in its infancy, and I have been privileged to be part of the development of the TOC/TP into the highly robust, powerful, insightful methodology it is today. The TOC/TP is a fundamental legacy of Goldratt, one that has developed, and will hopefully continue to develop into the future.

This is not really the place to spend time working through in great detail the individual tools of the TOC approach. Far better writers than I have already done that, and I would refer you to those people, in particular Lisa Scheinkopf and her book entitled *Thinking for a Change*, and others such as Bill Dettmer and Eli Schragenheim. What follows here is simply a brief overview of the key tools and their role in the overall scheme of the TOC approach. Each of these tools can be used on its own or in combination with others. They can form a holistic understanding of any organizational dimension, team dimension, or even of a life.

There are four key questions that the TP approach sets out to answer: what to change, what to change to, how to effect the change, and finally how to maintain, or sustain, the change. In trying to answer these questions the tools contained within the thinking processes were developed and comprise the following:

Current Reality Tree (CRT): This tool takes as its raw material the problems and issues that are affecting our life right now, what we call the Undesirable Effects (UDEs), and makes the point that wherever they exist it is possible, through the bonds of effect-cause-effect logic, to construct an analysis that can lead us to the core problem causing all those horrible effects. It is rooted in sufficiency logic, the use of the "if–then" dialogue. This is all about answering the question "what to change?" in our struggle to improve performance in whatever sphere.

Cloud: This is perhaps one of the real breakthrough tools that Eli Goldratt created. The simplicity of five boxes to capture the reality of any conflict is both brilliant and elegant. As a description of any conflict, whether one I wish to resolve or simply understand, this is without parallel in my mind. The rigor is also a key to the successful use of this tool. Simply filling in the boxes is rarely enough. The content of each box needs to be challenged, validated, and scrutinized before acceptance: the importance of understanding the logic of necessity is central to the use of the cloud technique, and also the surfacing of the assumptions that lie behind the existence of every cloud. From that, we hopefully move to understanding both why the conflict exists and what must be done to resolve the conflict, or which choice or decision to make that moves us forward on my journey. Not all clouds are to be resolved by breaking the dependency of the arrows; it is often enough to simply construct the cloud and listen to what it is saying. All clouds tell a story if we have the ears to hear and the patience to reflect on what they are trying to say.

Future Reality Tree (FRT): This is the place where we can paint the compelling picture. This is where we answer the question "what to change to?" and can then communicate the vision in terms that people can readily understand. Again through the use of sufficiency logic this picture can be constructed, shared, scrutinized, validated, and used as the basis for both communication about where we are going and also the starting point for any implementation project. Watching a group of people complete this analysis is usually very illuminating and also heartwarming. They have built a picture of what life might be like in their organization. They built it, they checked it, and own it. The desire to implement the changes it contains grows often to high levels of impatience!

Prerequisite Tree (PRT): But how to implement this wonderful picture is the next problem we face. We need a tool that enables us to tap into the intuition of our team or others in the organization, to try and help understand the obstacles that lie ahead, and use those obstacles as raw material for our implementation plan. The PRT is often described as the work breakdown structure of our plan, and that seems to my mind a reasonable description. Many find this tool particularly useful in trying to achieve ambitious objectives while tapping into the intuition of the team at the same time. This uses the logic of necessity and thus forces us to really think through that which is necessary for the objectives to be achieved.

Transition Tree (TRT): This is the step-by-step sequence of actions that enables us to not just see how to achieve the goal but also to measure our progress. We make course corrections if required without violating the primary task, which is the achievement of the intermediate objective from the PRT or any objective that we might deem to be of great importance within our team or our own life. Using the logic of sufficiency, I have used this technique to determine the individual steps I need to take in order to achieve the main staging posts on my journey. I have found it very valuable in checking the logic of the various training programs I have run over the years.

Negative Branch Reservation (NBR): There are always potential negative outcomes, however, and once more our intuition is strong, so here we can use the tool of the NBR to determine the impact this potential negative might have and then take the necessary steps to ensure it does not happen in reality. Again through the logic of sufficiency we can check the potential negative outcomes through the use of this tool effectively and quickly.

One final aspect of the TP relates to the scrutinizing process, which includes a set of checks to ensure that our logical understanding of the area being analyzed is robust and clear. Called the categories of legitimate reservation (CLRs), they comprise seven key checks on the logical constructs being created. They are described as "legitimate" categories, as we have numerous examples of reservations being raised about a logical construct that are less than complimentary about the person doing the analysis. In other words, scrutiny needs rules and that is what the CLR does—it provides rules for us to check our logical understanding. The seven categories are

1. Clarity reservation: This is more of a communication reservation: "seek to understand before seeking to be understood" as noted by Covey. This reservation should be used first when reviewing some-one else's work and last when reviewing your own. Examples of clarity statements are
   a. I do not understand the meaning of what you said.
   b. I do not see the significance of what you said.
   c. I do not understand the context of what you said.
   d. I do not understand the causality you claim exists.
2. Entity reservation: This reservation asks questions about the statement. It is a challenge to the entity itself, for example, is it complete? Does it contain causality? Is it two entities in one? Perhaps the listener does not believe it exists, and as a general rule, the simpler the statement the better the entity will be.
3. Causality reservation: This reservation asks questions about the arrow of cause and effect that links two entities. It suggests that the person doing the scrutiny has no issue with either statement, but cannot see that they are linked by the arrows of cause and effect.
4. Insufficiency reservation: This is the "logical and" reservation and simply asks for what else must be present for the effect to be present.
5. Additionality reservation: This is the "logical or" reservation, and this asks what else can lead to the same outcome without the presence of the first cause cited.
6. Predicted effect: If I am finding it difficult to gain consensus that my cause-and-effect logic is sound, then given the existing cause, can I predict a new effect with which to confirm the original analysis? If so, then I can have confidence about the whole logical structure created so far.
7. Tautology: This is simply the presence of circular logic and can usually be resolved through the use of predicted effect. If I accept the initial causality between an effect and, probably, an intangible cause, then I can also ask, if this intangible cause exists what other effect must be present and, if I find that, then I can have confidence about the first causal connection.

As part of the background to this book, I invited a number of people to reflect on their use of these tools over the years and how they perceived their value. The responses showed a wide level of knowledge and experience, with some of the tools more dominant than others. For some, the cloud was very powerful in determining causal relationships; for others the PRT offered both a tool for determining the way forward and also a communication tool for the same. It is interesting to note how many only used some of the tools and left others in the toolbox. This was partly because of their own needs and partly because of the way in which they had learned to use the whole of the toolset. For some the logic of the cloud was intuitive and powerful, and for others it was difficult and awkward; the same applied to the Current Reality Tree where some found it cumbersome and others enlightening. What I gained from this simple exercise was that it is critical to have a large toolbox containing many tools and over time develop the ability to use more of them, and add more to the box. The leaders who took part had all taken time to learn the tools and how to communicate both the "what" and the "why" of their use, thus helping others within the team to make genuine contributions.

However, this is not the place to discuss in any great detail both the thinking processes and the CLRs, suffice at this point that they exist and are central to any TP analysis. However, if you require a more detailed explanation of these tools, I suggest you work your way through some of the books already mentioned and perhaps attend a training program that allows you to both learn the whole set and practice their use so that you can do it for yourself.

THE USE OF THE TOC LEADERSHIP COACHING CYCLE

Over the past few years I have been developing the leadership coaching cycle as shown here. This cycle is drawn from work I have done in the past with similar approaches, notably Kolb, Rubin, and McIntyre (1974) and also Killen and de Beer (2006). I was keen to develop the use of the TOC/TP tools already described into a reflection process that helped me to coach the people I was working with at the time, using the basic structure of the TOC/TP but in a manner that was easily understood and described, both a story and a journey. I came up with this coaching cycle comprising five stations on the coaching journey, reflecting my interest in railways, and using the TOC/TP at each station (see Figure 2.1). Each station has a set of questions that needs to be answered using the process. I have been able to use this approach at all three levels, organization, team, and individual.

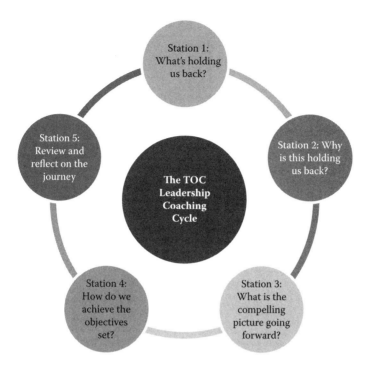

FIGURE 2.1
The TOC leadership coaching cycle.

Station 1: What's Holding Us Back?

This is the starting point for any understanding as to why we feel stuck in our journey. What is holding us back? Why are we not making more progress? Why is life so difficult? The first step in our analysis here involves *listening*. We take time to sit with people, to listen to them and capture the issues and problems they are facing, the hopes and desires they have, or perhaps once had, and from that we start to paint a picture of the environment in which they are living and working, which is possibly hurting them. Of course, all this is in the context of the goal and necessary conditions for the achievement of that goal, so these too have to be articulated. This is where I start to collect the UDEs: those statements of things that are present now and we wish they were not! I define the UDE as both an effect of something and a condition. So for example a common UDE in a production environment might be "Our level of work in progress (WIP) is very high." Now for the level of WIP to be high there has to be a cause—so what is that cause? At the same time it can be stated that this UDE has not just appeared overnight, so it is also a condition within the organization that does exist, and has existed over time. Sitting alongside the UDE statement there are actions that are being undertaken, and these too need to be captured. People are constantly taking actions that may be an attempt to remove the UDE, may be an attempt to work around the UDE, may be an action that tries to both address the UDE and seek to achieve the necessary condition the UDE jeopardizes; what is key here is to capture the action, or actions, and keep them for the analysis which follows. So using our example of high levels of WIP, the necessary condition that such an UDE violates might be delivery performance, and the actions required to try to achieve a high level of delivery performance might include expediting, which usually entails trying to pull the late order forward—usually at the expense of other orders!

Station 2: Why Is This Holding Us Back?

This question cannot be answered by a simple intuitive reaction. If we are really serious, we need to apply some real analytical tools. The reason for this level of rigor is that we have found, over the last twenty years or so, that in a complex situation, in an environment where there seems to be a very high level of complexity in everything, the need to find simplicity is paramount, the inherent simplicity that lies in all complex environments. This step asks a simple question: "What do we have to change (in order to move forward)?" At the end of this step, the key barriers to progress are known—but we are not done yet! So the status at the end of the second station is that, through careful communication, a high degree of consensus is achieved about the core problem most affecting the team and the organization, and there is a desire to do something about that problem.

Station 3: What Is the Compelling Picture Going Forward?

Once the consensus on the problem that is holding us back has been achieved, the next step is to gain consensus on the benefits of the solution to all the people involved, and I do mean all! This is where the whole concept of a win-win solution is fundamental; if anyone feels they are going to lose out at this point, they will find the capacity to stop it if they can or simply make it very difficult if they can't. This third station focuses on painting the picture of where we want to get to—the answer to the question "what to change to?" Based on the description of the problems and issues, can we now develop a structured picture of what the future might look like if we can break free from where we are? This picture is then submitted to scrutiny in order to have confidence that this is actually the future state we would really like to have in our possession. If we have captured all the UDEs, then we have also captured the equivalent Desirable Effects (DEs). So it is possible to paint an outline picture using just the DEs. However, they will raise questions about the solution that either challenge the benefits or the direction. This is where it pays handsomely to listen and take note: Do not under any circumstances challenge what is being said; their perception of reality is such that they will not listen to you, especially if you decide to take them on! Of course you might enjoy the fight, but your ability to lead has probably gone, so more discussion is needed if the picture is to gain any agreement and support. Changes will be needed to the current situation, the current condition, and those changes will involve understanding the choices that are open and those that are not. It will mean understanding the consequences of each choice in order to make a proper decision and the choice so made must lead to the achievement of the DEs, hence the need once more for rigor in our analysis. The status at the end of the third station is that all those within the team and the organization have reached a point of consensus about both the direction of the solution and the benefits that solution brings to all.

Station 4: How Do We Achieve the Objectives Set?

So what is stopping us? There will always be obstacles to the achievement of the goal, and the necessary conditions, so we need to surface them and deal with them. But we are not going to do this in an ad hoc manner, rather in a structured and logical manner that gives us confidence that when we start the journey we will arrive at the destination. That we can put in milestones that enable us to see progress, which in itself gives confidence that we are on the right pathway. It is crucial at this stage to tap into the intuition of the people within the organization. What this time is offering you is a unique insight into the obstacles people see coming toward them, the things that stop the solution from being implemented in the first place. They will speak in terms of obstacles, so listen carefully, have someone else capture the comments being made, thank them for their contribution, value that contribution, and give recognition and thanks to those who do raise issues; they are already joining with you on the journey. There is another form of reservation that often comes up at this point: These are negative consequences of successfully implementing the solution. Note that these are always negative outcomes of completing the implementation successfully and then it, whatever "it" might be, hits, and the result is a solution that promised much and delivers very little except additional headaches. So if you have been paying attention you now have two types of reservation—obstacles and potential negative outcomes—and as you have captured them you are able to deal with them straightaway.

People are to be encouraged to speak out, to voice their fears, the reasons why the solution might fail, and also any potential negatives that the proposers of the solution fail to spot in their enthusiasm.

This station is all about the "how to implement the solution" questions. How to develop a robust implementation plan? How to determine the resources needed? How to understand the sequencing of the tasks and the many other questions such planning demands? And the final step here is to simply implement the plan, make it happen, check the measures, and ask, did we arrive where we expected to arrive, and if not why not? Did we have to make course corrections on the way? The status at the end of the fourth station is that all reservations about the solution have been fully aired and the necessary actions determined that both allow for the full implementation of that solution, and a closing of the performance gap. At this stage the choices have been fully understood, the preferred choice noted and agreed, and all consequences, as far as can be known, noted. The decision can now be made to make that choice and implement all the decisions that follow. The tools we use from the TOC toolset are, for obstacles, the Prerequisite Tree (PRT), and for potential negative outcomes, the Negative Branch Reservation (NBR). We simply use the appropriate tool and move on. Once we have covered all the obstacles and the potential negatives, we will have dealt with all the reservations of the team and are ready to move to the final step—make it happen. For this we simply ensure that the actions that have been determined, those that take us from where we are right now to where we want to be as a result of implementing the solution, are completed. We execute each of the actions in the sequence as defined by another of the TOC tools, the Transition Tree (TRT), and using our implementation measurements, we are able to monitor progress toward completion of the solution, and also both the removal of the UDEs we started with, and the arrival of the DEs, which is what we have been after all along. Having come this far it is simple to then check the performance gap to see if it has closed and if so by how much. Has the gap closed, do we still need to continue with our analysis, in which case we go round the loop once more, and at the same time we take time to reflect on the journey to date, review what we did and in doing so, help to create the learning organization.

Station 5: Review and Reflect on the Journey

This is a crucial step. We need to look back and reflect on the journey. We may have successfully completed the implementation, or not! We may be still nearing the end of the journey and the expected results are not yet ours. Figure 2.2 shows the process I have been working with based on work done by Killen and de Beer for the process of Theological Reflection. In my use of the approach, I am focusing primarily on leadership and the experiences that leaders go through when trying to lead their team.

Many people dismiss the importance and time given to this activity; however there is still the need to recognize and practice both the time and place for reflection. What have we learned along the way? Did we have any problems and issues that arose during the journey that we did not

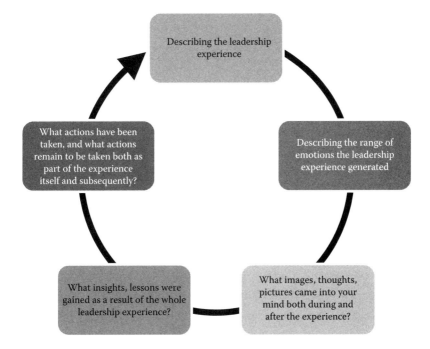

FIGURE 2.2
The process of reflection.

anticipate at the start? Have we changed our view of the goal, is it still the goal or perhaps do we now feel there is a larger goal that now lies before us? To do this, we invite those we are working with to keep a simple journal in order to help with this looking back, and thus quickly identify any constraints that appeared on the journey, the course corrections noted above, and also the good points that were achieved. This whole process helps to create more stories for the team and the organization. It will be marked by symbols, both of success and failure, symbols that enhance the myths and legends of the organization, and serve to enshrine the worldview of the organization. In this way the worldview of the team and the individuals is enhanced. Station 5 is critical for the success of this approach as without it there is no closure of the loop, no feedback system, and no opportunity to learn from the whole experience.

Thus using the coaching cycle in combination with the toolset of the TOC provides any leader with a powerful approach for closing the performance gap. In so doing, I have found the following:

1. It is important for the key leaders within the organization to check the direction of the company, the goal, and necessary conditions.
2. Examining the choices, the decisions, and the changes that these require to be successful and developing clear strategies to do so, including metrics, is crucial.
3. It is essential to work with the team, carrying out the analyses contained within the coaching cycle and, in particular, painting the compelling picture that those within the wider organization can adopt for themselves thus creating win-win solutions to problems that people can readily sign up to.
4. It is vital to coach those around the leaders, working with them to determine what is needed to get them on board, addressing issues rather than running roughshod over them.
5. Being prepared to work with an external coach who can ask the awkward questions, who is not supposed to know; but rather to ask the question "why," can be enormously helpful.

This is not a comprehensive coverage of the subject matter, but it does reflect much of what I have found on my own journey with clients drawn from around the world, and may be of significance to you. I will return to the application of the coaching cycle later in the book. So now let's move to the starting point for most TOC/TP analysis and certainly the starting point of our coaching cycle: the Undesirable Effect or UDE.

WHAT ARE UNDESIRABLE EFFECTS (UDEs), AND WHY ARE THEY IMPORTANT?

Over the years in which I have been active in using the TOC approach for coaching, I have set out to capture the problems and issues that are affecting the people with whom I am working. The common way to describe these issues in the TOC context is the use of the term Undesirable Effect, or UDE. Over the years, many analyses have been carried out using the UDEs of the area being addressed and analyzed, as the raw material for both understanding the issues and then to delving down to the core area to determine those unique causal factors that in fact are the primary causal factors for most of the UDEs that exist. But what are UDEs? They are the problems or issues that really bother us and need to be removed. I once described them as "midges," those delightful little beasties that reside in Scotland and give both visitors and locals such an interesting time! UDEs do require careful verbalization however, because if they are weak then they may not reveal their true nature.

My favorite example of a non-UDE was given to me many years ago during a ten-day TP program I was running at the time. One of the people attending put forward, with all sincerity and not a little passion, the following statement, claiming it was a major UDE and needed to be resolved. He wrote on the whiteboard "communication is poor" and then sat down. I asked the rest of the class if they understood, and agreed, with the UDE, and they did. However, when I asked just what was meant by the statement, i.e., a clarity reservation, I received five or six examples of communication and a similar number of meanings for the word "poor." I suggested that the only conclusion I could draw from the UDE statement was that whatever the issue was related to communication and its state, it was at least present tense as signified by the word "is." The debate however had taken the class to a much better understanding not just of the reality of the UDE being discussed, which was in fact about six UDEs altogether, but also the rigor that goes into the validation of an UDE.

WHAT ARE THE CRITERIA FOR
DETERMINING A GOOD UDE?

There are a number of key aspects that help us to understand and write clearly the UDE affecting us right now. They are part of our current situation right now, not last year, or once upon a time, or almost certainly going to occur tomorrow—they are present tense now, and have been present tense for a while, and will remain present tense into the future. They annoy us, have annoyed us for a while, and will continue to annoy us into the future, but it is always present tense annoyance that counts. They take up our time, now, and time we would rather spend on much more important aspects of our work; they should have been addressed some time ago, but that did not happen, and if nothing is done now, this time-stealing will continue into the future. They are negative, whether in truth or just a perception does not matter; it is enough that the UDE is seen as negative for it to be negative.

Negative is defined as anything "negative" in the eyes of the person citing the UDE to be of sufficient importance to meet the definition of an UDE. UDEs are symptoms of a deeper problem, although this is not always recognized; indeed I have been in many organizations with many projects underway simply trying to remove a single UDE per project. This happens when no one recognizes that an UDE has as the last word "effect" and therefore must be caused by something. So what is causing the UDE must be the key question, and that requires further analysis.

Is it an entity? It is strange over the years how many people have thought that just a word or two is sufficient for anyone to grasp the UDE, and that every UDE must be something that can be properly defined and in some cases seen or felt. It has to "be" something, not an abstract thought lying outside of any form of reality. Hence is it real, and remember perception of reality is just as valid as reality itself. This does not contradict the notion of something abstract; simply if my perception is that this thing, this effect, I am looking at right now is described in this way, then that is good enough. The next aspect relates to the ownership: is it negative in the mind of the owner, the person who has to deal with the UDE? Is it negative in the mind of the group? Either way, the UDE stands. Is it within the proposer's area of responsibility? This seems unimportant for some people, but is in fact very important. It is great to find UDEs that lie outside your span of control or influence and then sit back feeling comfortable as the UDEs holding you back are not yours to deal with but for someone else to address. That way you have no responsibility over addressing the UDE, and you can point the finger at someone else to fix it. The reality of course is that there are always UDEs in your area of responsibility, and if you don't identify them, or admit to them, other members of the team will always help! Is the UDE considered to be of sufficient importance to seek to remove it? If not then why are you putting it forward as an UDE? Importance is often defined as being related to the goal and/or the necessary conditions that deliver the goal, and this works at every level, personal, team, and organization. Does it reduce our capability? Is it a single item? Does it contain causality?

WHAT DOES A UDE COST?

For every UDE, there is a price and not just a financial one. It is key that if at all possible we can identify and set a value to the ongoing existence to the UDE should it not be removed. For one client, we added up the UDEs being addressed and the sum was over $7.5 M per year. Each UDE included in the analysis had a cost, and this turned out to be in the region of $500 to $5,000 per month, or per week in some cases. Of course across the global organization they soon added up! We try to quantify the real money lost, never the cost accounting allocations that cause so many problems. This is about real money lost, which should never have left the organization: money for additional labor when we already had enough, for outsourcing when we could have made it inside, for expediting when we should have delivered on time, in-full, and right the first time, and so on. Then, when we have covered the real money measurements, we can use the nonfinancial measures such as when our Due Date Performance (DDP) is less than 80 percent and try to quantify that perhaps in terms of lost sales, or additional costs to try and get the product or service to the client as close to the promised time as possible.

A CASE STUDY FROM THE WORLD OF THE MANUFACTURING INDUSTRY

This is a simple case study drawn from the world of manufacturing and involving a small company of about 150 people making precision parts for a wide range of clients in industries such as aerospace, automobile, pharmaceutical, and healthcare. They are a successful company and at the time of the research project were keen to develop their manufacturing capability in order to take advantage of an upsurge in interest from existing clients and new clients who had found them and wanted to work with them. They already knew that their systems for manufacture were not able to allow them to take advantage of these opportunities and so invited me to work with them and help them to create a more robust platform for the future, secure the jobs of those already working there, and perhaps open up the possibility of recruitment in the future.

The senior team was keen both to lead this project themselves, and also to use the opportunity to encourage those lower down in the management team to develop their own leadership capability as this would be a necessary condition for growth and sustainability in the future. The project started with a simple mapping exercise throughout the whole of the company, checking the flow of material from raw to finished product and asking the same question of everyone, "what are your UDEs," this after having explained what a UDE is.

Beginning the Process of Developing a UDE

This is where I use the simple approach of writing into each box one of three UDEs chosen for my analysis as shown in the box. These draft UDEs are picked at random from the full set captured during the mapping process and following discussion with the people at each stage of the process, from taking the order through to shipping.

UDE 1—write in the description of the 1st UDE here: some job cards are released without the correct tooling information
UDE 2—write in the description of the 2nd UDE here: some drawings are supplied incomplete
UDE 3—write in the description of the 3rd UDE here: there is a high level of WIP in the print room

But writing each UDE into the box is rarely enough; I have spent many hours with people working through the UDEs they have written in the box, having to ask them for clarity again and again. I do have one helpful piece of information however—before I ask them to show me their UDEs I have also asked them to fill into another set of boxes the storyline for each UDE.

This usually comprises a paragraph or maybe two and contains the situation in which the UDE exists. This reflects back to the discussion about the use of "story" discussed earlier. In this part of the process what I have found is that in the storyline a great deal more information is presented. Often the real UDE resides in the storyline rather than in the UDE box, and often the description contains all the assumptions I need to help them build the cloud, which we will cover later. It is as if the process of writing the story unlocks the mind, enabling people to wax lyrical about the UDE, the context in which it sits, the effects it has. I often find that more than one UDE is discussed in a single storyline, and then reappears in a later storyline. This is really opening up the mind, and the mindset, in such a way as to give a much clearer insight to the causality that surrounds the UDE.

Storyline for UDE 1: In this case the job cards are the means by which progress is captured as the product goes through the manufacturing process. It is often needed quickly in order to ensure a swift delivery to a key client. It is common for the missing data to be inserted later in the process as it becomes available, The job cards are filled in by sales and then are set for the rest of the time the order is live. The data on the job card can change during the production process if the client requests a change or production considers the change is required due to other circumstances.

Storyline for UDE 2: This is when, in order to meet the requirements of a rush order, the drawings are delivered later. Sometimes the client has not signed off the drawing, but we want to make progress if at all possible, and to release before the drawings simply allows us to get going. Although the drawings are critical for production, it is accepted that in order to get ahead, releasing without the drawings only means that the order is live quicker. Changes do occur to the drawings during the time out on the shop floor.

Storyline for UDE 3: The level of WIP is growing in the print room. The order is released, and if there is anything missing or changes are being made, then the print room is often where the order is held, and this all adds to the WIP level. Sometimes orders can get ahead of other orders at this point, and it is where we can also try to be more efficient with the use of equipment later in the process. Much expediting is seen here, changing the priorities.

At this point I am usually able to work with the person and to upgrade the UDE placed in the relevant box, and once we are both satisfied that the three UDEs have captured what the person is experiencing right now, we can safely move to the next stage. I should point out that sometimes this process of writing up the UDEs to meet the criteria for the next stage can take about an hour or so, and many times much longer. I have been known to insist that more time is spent at this stage as it is the bedrock of what is to come, and any false logic, any lack of clarity, will really hurt later and may even lead to the wrong conclusions and the wrong solutions being developed and implemented.

It might seem that this time spent validating and sharpening the UDEs is slowing down the whole process, which is partly true; it does slow the process down, but for very good reason. The UDEs are the raw material of the process itself and any mistakes here can cost us dearly in the future. There is a lovely description as to why this is so important in David Ruelle's book, *Chance and Chaos* (1991, Chapter 7, pp. 39–40), when he examines aspects of Chaos Theory. He uses a term called "sensitive dependence on initial condition." Or to put in layman terms, a small change in the starting condition, may, and often does, have enormous impact on the outcome.

Thus if we are looking for a robust solution to the problems and issues preventing us from reaching out toward the goal, then the rigor of our analysis and the confidence we have in the core problem identified must be high. The solution is totally dependent on the causal analysis and if we are keen to succeed then we should invest time and effort at this vital stage. Often I have witnessed the implementation of a solution, often with a high level of investment, which fails simply because the rigor that the process demands was not applied.

So we now have three UDEs from our first case study, taken from a list of over twenty. They have been subjected the usual level of scrutiny and the storylines read and understood. We are now ready to ask two questions, what is the root cause of these three UDEs, and from that analysis, can we then answer the question "what to change?" It is fair to say at this point that most of the work contained within Station 1 of the Coaching Cycle has been completed, we know what appears to be holding us back, but the question "why?" remains.

REFERENCES AND FURTHER READING

Dettmer, H. W. *Goldratt's Theory of Constraints*. Milwaukee, WI: ASQC Quality Press, 1997.

Dettmer, H. W. *Breaking the Constraints to World-Class Performance*. Milwaukee, WI: ASQ Quality Press, 1998.

Goldratt, E. M. *It's Not Luck*. Aldershot, UK: Gower, 1995.

Killen, P. O., and J. de Beer. *The Art of Theological Reflection*. New York: Crossroad, 2006.

Kolb, D. A., I. M. Rubin, and J. M. McIntyre. *Organizational Psychology: An Experiential Approach*. Englewood Cliffs, NJ: Prentice-Hall, 1974.

Ruelle, D. *Chance and Chaos*. London: Penguin, 1991.

Scheinkopf, L. J. *Thinking for a Change*. Boca Raton, FL: St. Lucie Press, 1999.

Schragenheim, E. *Management Dilemmas*. Boca Raton, FL: St. Lucie Press, 1998.

Woeppel, M. J. *Manufacturer's Guide to Implementing the Theory of Constraints*. Boca Raton, FL: St. Lucie Press, 2001.

3

Gaining Consensus on the Problem

GAINING CONSENSUS ON WHAT TO CHANGE

The dominant theme in my story of leadership lies in the step that begins with answering the question "what is the problem?" Once this question is successfully answered, it is then possible to move to the second question, "what to change?" In terms of the Coaching Cycle, this represents a completion of Stations 1 and 2 and then the core of Station 3. In the years that I have studied the question of leadership, the ability to set the right course has dominated almost all the discussions I have had. But the right course depends on two pieces of information: a clear statement as to the destination, which in the context of this book, is the goal and the necessary conditions, coupled with a clear statement as to where we are now. Only if these two pieces of information are available, and correct, can the journey begin as these two dictate the direction. What remains are the choices we make about how to get there and perhaps before that, do we even want to go there. In our first case study, introduced in the Chapter 2, we went through the process by which our understanding of the issues holding us back from achieving the goal are first identified and understood—the UDEs and the context in which they exist. Now we need to use those UDEs to help us understand why they exist in the first place, as they are effects and therefore have a cause. As they all exist within the same context, the company, and the same environment and are subject to the same ways of managing, then it is reasonable to assume that there is a common cause, and if we can determine that common cause then we will have identified what needs to change in order to move the whole company forward. We need a tool that can use UDEs as raw material and substantially enhance our understanding of the context of the UDEs, the assumptions that lie behind them and hopefully give us the necessary focus in order to do something about them. Only when we can discern both what is holding us back from the goal, and why that constraint is present can we say we have completed Stations 1 and 2. To accomplish this we need a powerful analytical process, which thankfully the TOC Thinking Process (TP) is. The key tool from the TP toolset we are going to use here is called the "cloud."

GAINING AN UNDERSTANDING ABOUT "CLOUDS"

The idea of using five simple boxes to try and understand a conflict was first described by my friend Eli Goldratt. He used the term "evaporating cloud," having read the 1977 book by Robert Bach entitled *Illusions*, in which one of the characters attempts to eradicate clouds through the use of thinking. In fact, the term in the book is more akin to vaporizing clouds, which to my mind is stronger and more positive than evaporating clouds. Vaporizing involves a clear physical effort to achieve the task, whereas evaporating will happen over time anyway. But whether I prefer one title over another, the common term of "cloud" dominates, so I will go with that! So what does a cloud look like? It is simply five boxes connected in the way shown in Figure 3.1. The main boxes, entitled A, B, C, D, and D', make up the main structure of the cloud. The logical structure of the cloud is that of necessity.

Thus A is the objective of the cloud, and both B and C are the necessary conditions, needs that are both required for the objective to be realized. Although defined as necessary conditions, they are not always sufficient in themselves for the existence of the objective. In the same manner, D is the necessary condition for B, the "want" that justifies the need in the B box, and in the same manner D' is the necessary condition for C, the "want" that justifies the need in the C box. The conflict, or choice, exists between D and D'. It should be noted that neither B nor C should be in conflict; indeed as they are both necessary for the existence of the goal, they must also be read in a positive light.

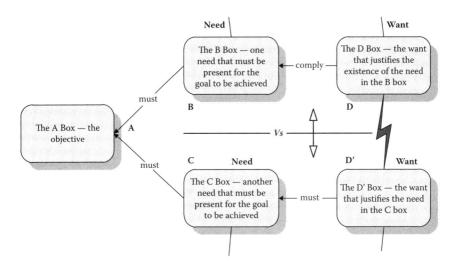

FIGURE 3.1
The basic cloud structure.

A DISCOURSE ON METHOD

There are, at least, two ways of writing the cloud associated with any one UDE—the situational and the behavioral. For the behavioral construction the essence is focusing on the actions that are being taken as a direct result of the existence of the UDE, hence the term *behavioral* (see Figure 3.2). The construction steps for this approach are the following the questions, starting with the B box:

> What need is jeopardized by the UDE (why is it an UDE)? **This is the B box.**
> What action must be taken to achieve need B? **This is the D box.**
> What need prevents you from doing D? **This is the C box.**
> What action must be taken to achieve C? **This is the D' box.**
> For what objective are B and C necessary conditions? **This is the A box.**
> D must jeopardize C, and D' must jeopardize B. **This is the cross-connection where the statement in the D box violates the existence or jeopardizes the statement in the C box, and the same for the D' and B boxes.**

We have found that leaders have to recognize the actions that are currently being taken by those around them that revolve around the

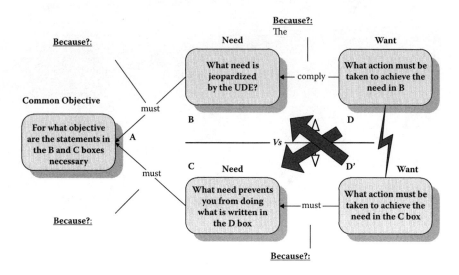

FIGURE 3.2
Behavioral cloud structure.

continued existence of an UDE. In our research, we have found that many people are taking three different types of action here. The first relates to actions being taken as a direct result of the status or condition related to the UDE and the impact it has upon performance, which often simply reinforces the current state. The second set of actions are those that are trying, by working around the UDE, to address the current state, and the third set are those actions that are trying to change the current state to that desired in order to achieve the goal. This construction method also places a high degree of importance on the impact actions have on the needs, the cross-connections. It is implicit in the analysis of the cloud that actions are impacting negatively the needs as written in the C and B boxes.

The second type of cloud is the situational (see Figure 3.3). This is based around the notion of seeing an UDE as a condition, a status point derived from the system being reviewed. The situational approach sees the UDE as something which I have but most certainly do not want.

The two approaches described here, behavioral and situational, can both be considered when trying to address an UDE. Which to use is a choice, and should remain so. The leader has to choose, as both are effective in helping to answer the question "what to change?" and there will be times when both are used. As a leader myself, I want to retain the widest range of tools possible, without any exclusion, thus allowing

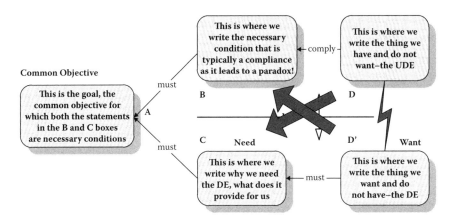

FIGURE 3.3
Situational cloud structure.

maximum flexibility in executing the task and achieving the objective. In both cases, the outcome should be, and in my experience is, the same. The rigor of both is good, and the judge of one over the other lies in the achievement of the objective, which is the real judge of any tool, and personal preference.

So let's examine how we construct the situational UDE cloud. The starting point is typically the statements of the condition or status that we are most familiar with, the Undesirable Effect (UDE). I start with the two statements that I know a great deal about already, the UDE and its corollary, the Desirable Effect (DE). So I start with the D box and fill in there the answer to the question as shown (what is the thing we have and do not want), which should be the statement of the UDE already defined. I can then follow this with the DE statement in the D' box (what is it we want and do not have) and make sure that the way I have written them at least shows they are in conflict. Then, why do we need the DE, the reason why I want the DE, the need that makes the statement in the D' box so critical, so necessary—this is the C box. This is followed by stating the goal, which is also the common objective for which the statements written in the B and C boxes are necessary conditions, and this is what goes in the A box.

In my experience, the filling in of these four boxes does not create too many problems, some revision perhaps, but usually only just to improve the way it reads rather than any major changes of understanding or content. Now it is the turn of the B box, which always seems to be more problematic. It is a paradox after all: The B box statement is a necessary condition, a statement of something that if it is not present means that the goal is not achievable, not able to be present. So in trying to answer the question set within this box, what we are seeking is a statement that tries to deliver the goal and at the same time results in the presence of the UDE. So in trying to achieve the goal I end up with an UDE! Asking why this is so is the reason we then, after completion of the cloud itself, move to surfacing the assumptions that lie behind each of the arrows, for it is here that we can discover the reasons for the existence of not just one UDE but perhaps all of them—which means we have answered the question "why?"

Once the cloud has been verbalized in this way, the next stage is to ensure that the logic holds true by reading the cloud aloud and amending the verbalization where necessary. This is a necessary step in the validation of the cloud and applies to either type, situational or behavioral. We need to validate the cloud by reading it in the correct manner. To do this we start by saying: "**In order to** (say what is written in the A box) **we/I must** (say what is written in the C box)"; pause and reflect, did it read correctly? Did it sound right? Intuition is wonderful here, so listen to that inner voice and correct the statements, making sure that at the same time the primary meaning is not lost. This is all about gaining greater clarity. Once you are happy with the A-to-C logic, move to the C to D' by saying "**in order to** (say what is written in the C box) **I/we must** (say what is written in the D' box)" and then repeat the process of validation as used for the previous arrow, and rewrite if necessary.

We are now ready to move to the next step, which is to do the same for the top line beginning with the A box once and using the same phrase: "**in order to** (the statement in the A box) **I must** (say what is written in the B box)," validate as before, and then say "**in order to** (say the B box) **I must** (say what is written in the D box)," and again validate. Once the verbalization of the cloud is clear and any rewrites completed, the next step is to surface the assumptions that lie beneath every arrow. This is done by adding the word "because" after the phrases emphasized in the previous paragraph. For example "**In order to** *have (C)* **I must** *have (D')* **because** . . ." The assumptions that are surfaced are then placed in the appropriate box. I then check for cross-connection, the impact the statement in the D' box has upon the statement in the B box, and similarly for the impact of D upon C. Once I have checked this final step, the cloud is now completed.

CASE STUDY 1: SMALL-SCALE MANUFACTURING

Now we return to the case study we explored at the end of Chapter 2 with the three defined UDEs and their respective storylines. This followed an exercise to fully map the process from receipt of order to shipping it to the client. During the time the mapping exercise was taking place, the opportunity was taken to compile a list of the daily problems and issues that people were dealing with. These UDEs were then placed into the map at the place they were first identified. This analysis was then validated first by the people working in the areas that gave us the UDEs and then further by the manager of the function. This led to us having confidence that these UDEs represented the reality people were facing each and every day.

This is the first UDE: **Some job cards are released without the correct tooling information** and formed the basis for the initial investigation. I have completed the whole of the UDE in the manner described above, including the surfacing of the assumptions. The UDE was placed into the relevant box and then the rest of the cloud constructed in the sequence D–D'–C–A–B followed by surfacing the assumptions. The cloud was then checked through the process of reading and confirming that it made sense, both to those who created it and those who have to live with it. Once any changes proposed had been taken into account and the cloud upgraded, this marked the end of this first step of analysis for the first UDE (see Figure 3.4). So reading the cloud we would say: **In order to** *deliver all product 100 percent on time and in full, right the first time,* **we must** *have accurate manufacture of all the client components* **because …**" and then read the assumptions listed under the A–C arrow. We can read the next bit, from C–D': "**in order to** *have accurate manufacture of all the client components* **we must have** *all the job cards released with the correct tooling information* **because . . . ,**" and again read the assumptions listed for the C–D' arrow. Then return to the A box and start again this time reading the top line, "**in order to** *deliver all product 100 percent on time and in full, right the first time,* **we must** *work to the existing process of job card creation* **because . . .**" and once more read the relevant assumptions under the A–B arrow. Finally we read from the B box to the D box, "**in order to** *work to the existing process of job card creation* **we are complying with** *the release of the job cards without the correct tooling information,* **because . . .**" and here we read of the reasons, the assumptions, as to why the UDE written in the D box continues to exist.

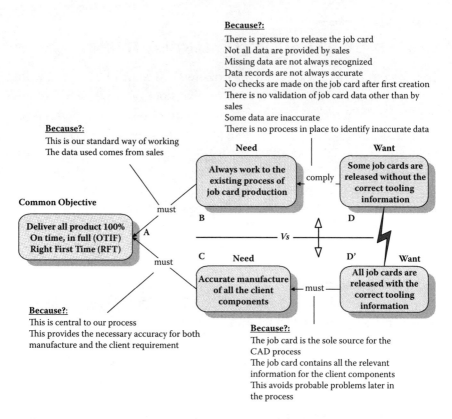

Because?:
There is pressure to release the job card
Not all data are provided by sales
Missing data are not always recognized
Data records are not always accurate
No checks are made on the job card after first creation
There is no validation of job card data other than by sales
Some data are inaccurate
There is no process in place to identify inaccurate data

Because?:
This is our standard way of working
The data used comes from sales

Need

Always work to the existing process of job card production

Want

Some job cards are released without the correct tooling information

comply

Common Objective

Deliver all product 100% On time, in full (OTIF) Right First Time (RFT)

must

B

Vs

D

A

C

Need

Accurate manufacture of all the client components

must

D'

Want

All job cards are released with the correct tooling information

must

Because?:
This is central to our process
This provides the necessary accuracy for both manufacture and the client requirement

Because?:
The job card is the sole source for the CAD process
The job card contains all the relevant information for the client components
This avoids probable problems later in the process

FIGURE 3.4
First UDE cloud.

This in itself is an illuminating process, and often people say at this point that there are some assumptions here that are not correct, that there are some that are no longer true, that some can and should be changed. However, I usually stop them at this point and ask them to move to the next UDE and construct the second UDE cloud and so on. Thus our next step is to add UDEs two and three as clouds, and these are shown in Figures 3.5 and 3.7. They are read in the same way as for the first cloud, and the assumptions read and understood. It is important that each cloud is treated as stand-alone so that the process is not skewed by the intuition being gained through the process of construction. In this way it is possible to keep, as best as is possible, an open mind as to the global picture being created with each successive cloud.

The second UDE is: **Some drawings are supplied incomplete.**

So for the second cloud we read that "**in order to** *achieve the delivery of all product 100 percent on time and right first time* **we must** *manufacture*

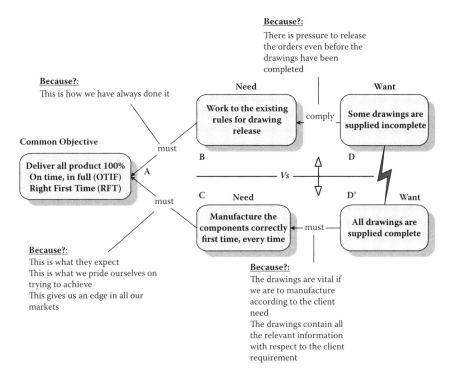

Because?:
There is pressure to release the orders even before the drawings have been completed

Because?:
This is how we have always done it

Need

Work to the existing rules for drawing release

Want

Some drawings are supplied incomplete

comply

B

D

Common Objective

Deliver all product 100% On time, in full (OTIF) Right First Time (RFT)

A

must

Vs

C **Need**

Manufacture the components correctly first time, every time

must

D' **Want**

All drawings are supplied complete

must

Because?:
This is what they expect
This is what we pride ourselves on trying to achieve
This gives us an edge in all our markets

Because?:
The drawings are vital if we are to manufacture according to the client need
The drawings contain all the relevant information with respect to the client requirement

FIGURE 3.5
Second UDE cloud.

the components correctly first time and every time, and **in order to** *manufacture the components correctly first time and every time* **we must have** *all drawings supplied complete to production,"* and the assumptions are there so that we understand the logic of this part of the cloud.

Then turning to the top line we read that, "**In order to** *deliver all products on time, in full, right the first time,* **we must** *work to the existing rules for drawing release* and **in complying with** that requirement *some drawings are supplied incomplete,"* and again the assumptions are noted. It is at this point, as the second UDE is both read and understood, that the other aspect of a cloud comes into focus, the cross-connection (see Figure 3.6). If the statement in the D box is examined closely, it is possible to ask a simple question which is, "What is the impact of the statement contained in the D box upon the statement written in the C box?"

I have found that understanding the impact and significance of the cross-connection reinforces the issues and is a very powerful way of understanding the devastating impact the unresolved conflict has on the individuals, the team, and the organization. This is also where the desire

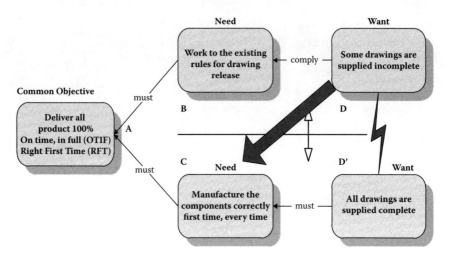

FIGURE 3.6
Third UDE cloud.

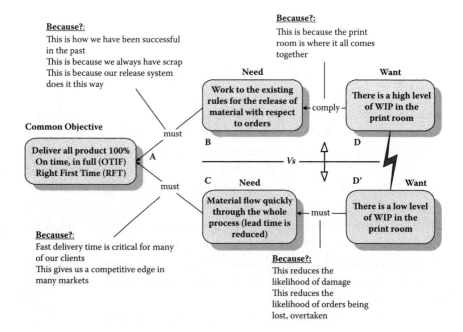

FIGURE 3.7
Cross-connection second UDE cloud.

to deal once and for all with the conflict is heightened. From this cloud we can see that our ability to manufacture components correctly must be at risk as long as the drawings are supplied incomplete. It might be odd, but this relationship, UDE to a necessary condition for the goal, is often completely overlooked, or if known then the real impact remains hidden. The same impact can also be seen when we examine the effect of the statement in the D' box on the B box where the achievement of the DE starts to challenge just why the current system does not do what was expected of it. This is also very much in line with what W. Edwards Deming (1986) argued when he reminded us that rarely are people to blame for nonconformance, but the system almost certainly is. So let's move to the final cloud of this part of our analysis—the third UDE cloud (see Figure 3.6).

The third UDE is: **There is a high level of WIP in the print room.**

The cloud is constructed and read in the same way as before, and the assumptions are then surfaced and inserted, checked, and finally we can ask about the impact of the cross-connection between the D box and the C box and the D' to the B box. We can also draw conclusions about how material can or cannot flow quickly when there is a high level of WIP at one point, or indeed spread around the production floor.

So what we have done so far is to take three UDEs and create three clouds, check them, surface the assumptions for each, and think about the story these three clouds tell us. I often find at this point that those who have lived the experience the clouds represent are only too well aware of the story being described in each of the clouds and the daily responses to that story. This is both a story that tries to speak of the journey toward the objective of the organization, as well as telling of the daily strife that is going on in order to achieve that objective. The gap in execution that everyone is only too well aware of is now clear to all, but we are not finished yet.

There remains a nagging doubt: Is this it or is there more to come? This is where the logic of the cloud enters with great force. We have determined the UDEs and the conflicts they create between what we want and what we have, so is there a deeper cause, still unseen? It is to answer this question that we can now turn our attention. Every UDE chosen comes from the same logical reality, and therefore we should be able to combine the three UDE clouds into one single, comprehensive, composite cloud and perhaps in so doing we will discover a deeper causality and thus the core driver for the chosen UDEs. To do this we write each of the UDEs into the boxes as shown in Figure 3.8. And we then write in the box a statement

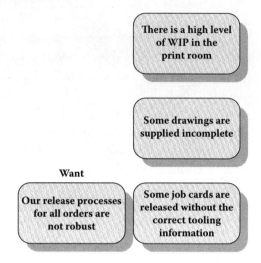

FIGURE 3.8
Creating the composite cloud—D.

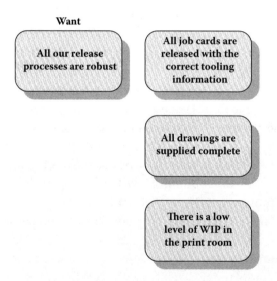

FIGURE 3.9
Creating the composite cloud—D'.

that captures the three individual statements as one. Figure 3.8 shows how this is done for the UDE statements, and Figure 3.9 for the DE statements.

We then continue around the remaining boxes of the new cloud, doing the same as for the D and D' boxes, until we have created a new cloud shown in Figure 3.10.

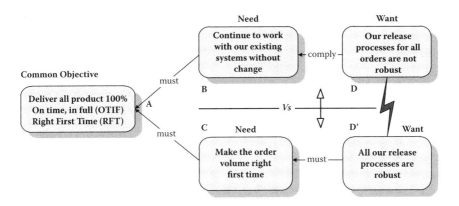

FIGURE 3.10
The composite cloud.

We can then read the cloud as before, so in this case, "**in order to** *deliver all product 100 percent on time, in full and right first time,* **I need to** *make the order volume right first time,* and **in order** *to make the order volume right first time* **I must have** *all our release processes are robust.*" Then, returning to the A box continue by saying, "**in order to** *deliver all product 100 percent on time, in full and right first time,* **I must** *continue to work with our existing systems without change* and **in continuing** *with the existing systems without change* **I must continue to comply** *with our release processes for all products are not robust.*" We read this and follow the normal process of validation and then, when satisfied with the text, continue to surface assumptions. We expect that all previous assumptions still work, but there are often new assumptions that this new understanding allows me to see. We can then use the cross-connection and see if that confirms the story we already know a great deal about.

There is one final step in this process of discovery about answering the question "what to change," and that is to communicate the analysis in such a way that all can see what is being presented and comment, ask questions, and maybe even give a better phrase that everyone agrees with. In this way we gain consensus on the problems and also see clearly the impact of doing nothing. The communication of the analysis takes us to the use of another tool within with TP toolset the Communication Current Reality Tree (CCRT).

Whereas the cloud uses the logic of necessity, the CCRT uses the logic of sufficiency through the use of "If...then" statements. We start with the cloud statements, taken from the composite cloud, and then begin the process of construction, using appropriate assumptions to do so. The CCRT for this analysis is shown in Figure 3.11. The ellipses are the "logical and" statements and the whole logical structure is read in the following way.

Starting at the bottom, "**if** *I want to deliver all product 100 percent on time, in full (OTIF) right first time (RFT)* **and if** *Fast Delivery time is critical for many of our clients* (this is an assumption surfaced earlier), **then** *we must make the order volume right first time.*" We pause, and this allows people to take that in before continuing, "**if** *we must make the order volume right first time,* **and if** *the job card contains all the relevant information for the client components,* **then** *we must ensure that all our releases processes are robust.*" OK so far, but now we have to stop and return to the beginning and go up the left-hand side of our logical structure. So "**if** *we want to deliver all product 100 percent on time, in full (OTIF) right first*

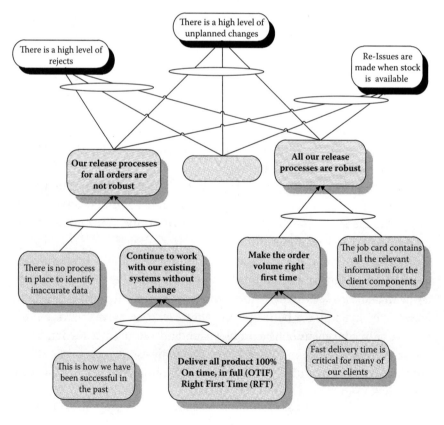

FIGURE 3.11
The CCRT.

time (RFT) **and if** *this is how we have been successful in the past,* **then** *we continue to work with our existing systems without change.* Continuing, we then read "**if** *we continue to work with our existing systems without change* **and if** *there is no process in place to identify inaccurate data,* **then** *our release processes for all orders are not robust.*" So here is the conflict, we seek to manage our business with robust release processes while at the same time continuing with the existing, nonrobust systems *because* today, there is no alternative system in place, we have not invested any time in developing a new system, we do not have the skills to develop such a system, we do not know where to start to create such a system, and so on. Suddenly, keeping the two statements from the composite cloud apart, we can work our way through a whole raft of assumptions that will only maintain the conflict into the future. We can even predict the logical connection to other UDEs, as shown in Figure 3.11, which then starts to show that this core conflict is not just the cause of the three UDEs chosen at the start but at least another three more such as "high level of rejects," "high level of unplanned changes," and finally "reissues are made when Finished Good Stock is available." We could also return to the original UDE list which contains far more than six or seven UDEs and keep asking the same question, does this analysis connect to a substantial proportion of the UDEs captured to date, and if the answer is yes then we have been able to construct an important logical understanding of the predicament the company is in. I have brought myself, as leader, to an understanding of the issues and indeed the core issue affecting the performance of the business and can then bring the members of the team, followed by the wider team, to the same understanding. All this is necessary in order to gain consensus on the problem, the core problem, right now, holding us back from achieving the goal. Once that has been achieved then we can start to ask the next set of questions. If this conflict remains unresolved, then the current UDEs will continue to give me serious cause for concern and perhaps lead to the company failing to meet the goal and perhaps going out of business altogether. This is where leadership comes in. This is where I have found that choices have to be made and not always easy choices. So at this step we have completed the work required in Stations 1 and 2, and we know what is holding us back and why. We can see the devastating impact of the UDEs and the core conflict that drives all of the current problems and issues. We can determine the DEs from this analysis so we have a glimpse of what the future might look like, but it is only a glimpse, not a fully developed picture as yet, and certainly not a compelling one.

But we can, through careful communication, gain the consensus we seek at this point.

So you might think that, faced with the conclusions that can be drawn from the analysis to date, the direction going forward should be clear, maybe not the detail, but at least the broad picture—so what happens next? Place yourself in the position of the leader of this company: what would you do, what choices do you have? Can you think about what should happen next? What is the range of choices and what implications, consequences, follow each choice you might make? What decisions follow each of the choices you are considering? Do any of these decisions create for you or your team members a problem, one that puts them into a conflict of subordination? Does any one single choice challenge a paradigm, your paradigm, a team member's paradigm? And what about the wider team, the other people who will be involved in the execution of the choice/decision if not the making of that choice or decision, will they be able to subordinate to the choice made? Think about this carefully, for this is the position many of the leaders I meet across many types of industry find themselves in, and this is what they have to resolve. In the next chapter, we will work our way through three more case studies to gain a real and hopefully deeper understanding of the importance of these two stations of the cycle.

REFERENCES AND FURTHER READING

Bach, R. *Illusions*. New York: Dell Publishing, 1977.
Deming, W. E. *Out of the Crisis*. Cambridge, MA: MIT Center for Advanced Engineering Study (CAES), 1986.

4

Case Studies to Help Us

**USE OF CASE STUDIES TO HELP US
UNDERSTAND THE PREDICAMENT OF
LEADERS IN ORGANIZATIONS TODAY**

I have been very fortunate over the years to have worked in a variety of
places, companies, and organizations, all of which gave me great satisfaction primarily because of the people I met. Their enthusiasm was heartwarming and especially so when all around them seemed to be collapsing!
I would like to use the following three case studies to illuminate further
the issues the leaders within each of these organizations were facing, and
later in the book I will reveal what happened in each case. The first two case
studies are drawn from the maintain and repair environment and the third
is from the healthcare environment. In each case, read through the story
that is told and then try to answer the questions set at the end. There is no
right or wrong answer, but I would like to feel that you will think about the
choices that each of the leaders had and then the decisions that would follow that choice. In all three cases, I intend to take you through the first two
stations of the coaching cycle and let you draw the compelling picture that
might follow the choice you make based on the analysis. Each case started
with the mapping of the flow and the capture of the current articulation
of the goal and necessary conditions. Once that had been accomplished,
the next step was to collect the Undesirable Effects (UDEs) and place them
on the map in order to determine just what was holding the organization
back, thus creating the performance gap, and why the gap existed. Once
this had been completed, the clouds of each UDE were constructed and

validated, complete with assumptions, and then the composite cloud constructed. The process continued with the Communication Current Reality Tree (CCRT) and then the identification of the key changes and the DEs such that the compelling picture could be developed.

I find Maintain and Repair Organizations (MROs) fascinating. Perhaps this is because the early years of my working life were spent in MRO with the Armed Forces (1965–1981) as a radar engineer repairing and maintaining radar equipment being used by the Royal Artillery. Whenever something broke we were under pressure to repair whatever it was as quickly as we could as the equipment could help to win a battle, save life, and protect our own troops; all good reasons at the time. From the outset, the goal of such an organization was made very clear: fast response, zero defect as a given, no question. Years later when the opportunity came for me to work in the MRO environment once more, I was keen to see how things had changed. Was the ability to turn around defective equipment now substantially enhanced since my time in MRO? Were the same measures still in use, for example Fast Turnaround Time (TAT) and Zero Defect? Was the ability of the supply chain to meet the demands of today up to the challenge? These and many more questions lay at the back of my mind as I started to work with two clients in MRO and from which the following case studies were derived.

CASE STUDY 1 FROM AN MRO ENVIRONMENT

This case study followed the usual practice of meeting the people involved and responsible for the area under review. This included a simple mapping of the key flows, both of material and information, and inviting the people within the team to tell their story. The stories captured contained a number of possible UDEs, all of which were validated and the storylines written. The UDEs contained here are those chosen by the team within the MRO facility and the analysis is their own work, although coaching was given.

UDE 1 from the first MRO environment: **There are often stock-outs of key lubricants within the warehouse**. This UDE was captured as we started to work our way through a series of mapping exercises all related to the MRO organization as a whole. The procedure outlined in Chapter 3 was followed—map, capture the UDE, check its position on the map, write the storyline, write the UDE out again, and check it with the person who

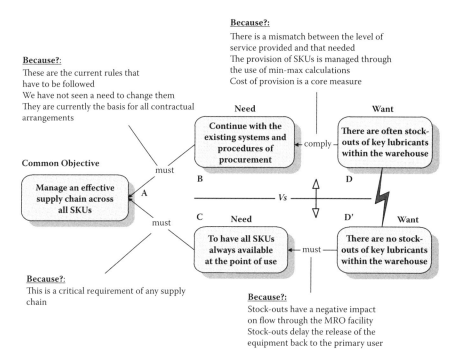

FIGURE 4.1
First MRO case study UDE cloud 1.

raised it for both validation and confirmation as to the accuracy of the UDE and the assumptions raised. Figure 4.1 depicts the cloud as validated by the key people involved.

In order to *manage an effective supply chain across all SKUs (Stock Keeping Unit)* **we must** *have all SKUs continually available at the Point of Use (or consumption),* **because** *this is a critical requirement of any supply chain.* **In order to** *have all SKUs always available at the point of use,* **there must be** *no stock-outs of key lubricants within the warehouse* **because** *stock-outs have a negative impact on flow through the MRO facility,* **because** *stock-outs delay the release of equipment back to the primary user.* However, **in order to** *manage an effective supply chain across all SKUs* **I must** *continue with the existing systems and procedures of procurement* **because** *these are the rules that are mandated throughout the organization,* **because** *there is no need to change these rules,* **because** *these rules are currently the basis for all contractual arrangements.* Therefore, **in continuing with** *the existing systems and procedures of procurement* **I have to comply** *with often having stock-outs of key lubricants within the warehouse,* **because** *there is a mismatch between the level of service provided and that needed,* **because** *the* *provision of the level of each SKU is managed through the use of min-max calculations,* **because** *the cost of provision is a core measure.*

So on the one hand, I want to have no stock-outs of these key lubricants as they are critical for much of the work that is being done within the MRO facility, while at the same time I am in the position of having to put up with stock-outs of these key lubricants because of the manner in which the supply chain is managed and measured. Checking the cross-connection confirms the negative impact the UDE has upon availability at the point of use, and the desired outcome of having sufficient lubricant violates the rules and procedures of the procurement process and the key measure of cost of supply. The problems created by the stock-out were not included in any of the core measures. The impact of the stock-outs was figured in another department, where a different set of measures were employed. In terms of behaviors, there was much expediting, over-ordering of the key lubricants and searching for the right lubricant in others areas within the MRO facility; if found, the lubricant then found its way to the bay in question, with "help."

So what about the next UDE: **Material (lubricant) is often supplied to the point of consumption close to, or just after, the "use by" date**.

Again this UDE was captured at the same time as UDE1, and the storyline was written and the cloud developed in the usual way, as shown in Figure 4.2. This time it reads, "**In order to** *manage an effective supply chain across all SKUs* **I must** *avoid the waste of (existing) SKU material (stock)* **because** *this adds to overall costs,* **because** *our supply should be Lean,* **because** *our budget is finite;* and **in order to** *avoid the waste of SKU material* **we must have** *the supply of that material well in advance of the 'use by' date,* **because** *this ensures that SKUs are used properly,* **because** *this avoids the likely costs of waste due to product being thrown away.* However, **in order to** *manage an effective supply chain across all SKUs* **we must** *continue with the existing systems and procedures of procurement* **because** *these are the current rules that have to be followed,* **because** *we have not seen a need to change them,* **because** *they (the rules) are currently the basis for all contractual arrangements.* And, **in complying** *with the existing systems and procedures for procurement,* **we have to comply with** *material often supplied after the 'use by' date,* **because** *there are often delays in the provision of the SKUs,* **because** *this is a function of the current process to replenish SKUs,* **because** *this is what happens when aggregates are used.*" As with the usual practice of checking the impact such a cloud can have, examining the cross-connection shows the consequence

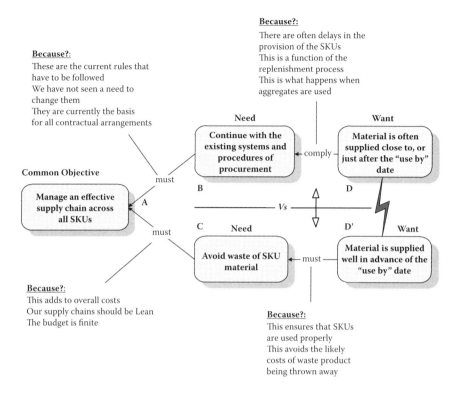

Because?:
There are often delays in the
provision of the SKUs
This is a function of the
replenishment process
This is what happens when
aggregates are used

Because?:
These are the current rules that
have to be followed
We have not seen a need to
change them
They are currently the basis
for all contractual arrangements

Need

**Continue with the
existing systems and
procedures of
procurement**

B

Want

**Material is often
supplied close to, or
just after the "use by"
date**

D

← comply ─

Common Objective

**Manage an effective
supply chain across
all SKUs**

A

must

must

Vs

C Need

**Avoid waste of SKU
material**

← must ─

D' Want

**Material is supplied
well in advance of the
"use by" date**

Because?:
This adds to overall costs
Our supply chains should be Lean
The budget is finite

Because?:
This ensures that SKUs
are used properly
This avoids the likely
costs of waste product
being thrown away

FIGURE 4.2
First MRO case study UDE cloud 2.

of having material, in this case lubricant, being supplied close to, or just after, the "use by" date in that it has to be thrown away, in line with the rules of such disposal, as it is no longer fit for purpose. When asked about the volume in which the lubricants were supplied, the consumption point only required small amounts, say a pint or so, but it was supplied in large containers each with some five-hundred gallons. The order to replenish that which had been used was only placed after a significant number of outlets for the lubricant, in aggregate, reached this economic order quantity. Therefore for an order to be accepted by the Original Equipment Manufacturer (OEM) supplier of lubricants, the process of aggregation was required in order to meet the requirement of an economic order quantity at the OEM. So, a number of consumption points would each be signaling what they had used and a central ordering point within the MRO facility would wait until there was sufficient demand to equal the order point requirement and then place the order. This in itself could take a considerable amount of time. Then once the order had been placed the supplier of the lubricant also aggregated the demand from all the possible outlets for that particular SKU, in other words, until there was sufficient demand to make that particular lubricant SKU; they would then manufacture and only then supply. Each MRO facility would then decant the lubricant into the amounts required at the points of consumption. By this time, the "use by" date was considerably closer than when the order from the consumption point was first registered. The same behaviors noted in response to UDE1 were also prevalent here, as might be expected.

The third UDE from this environment picked up on the level of expediting that was taking place within the MRO facility: **There is a significant amount of expediting in key SKUs**. In this case, the A, B, and C boxes remained the same as before, but the conflict as seen in D and D' was different (see Figure 4.3).

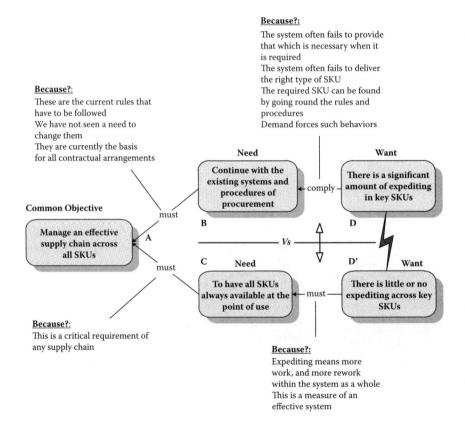

FIGURE 4.3
First MRO case study UDE cloud 3.

So, read the cloud as follows: "**In order to** *manage an effective supply chain across all SKUs* **we must have** *all SKUs available at the point of use,* **because** *this is a critical requirement of any supply chain.* **In order to** *have all SKUs available at the point of use* **there must be** *little or no expediting across key SKUs,* **because** *expediting means more work, and more rework within the system as whole,* **because** *this is a measure of an effective system.* However, **in order to** *manage an effective supply chain across all SKUs* **we must** *continue with the existing systems and procedures for procurement,* **because** *these are the current rules and must be followed,* **because** *we have not seen a need to change them (the rules),* **because** *they are currently the basis for all contractual arrangements,* and **in complying** *with those existing systems and procedures for procurement* **there is** *a significant amount of expediting in key SKUs* **because** *the system often fails to provide that which is necessary when it is required,* **because** *the system often fails to deliver the right type of SKU,* **because** *the required SKU can be found by going round the rules and procedures,* **because** *the demand forces such behaviors.*" Again the cloud was validated by the MRO team, the assumptions checked, and the cross-connections examined. The consensus was that the level of expediting was high, going to become even higher, and was causing all manner of disruption in the supply chain and dysfunctional behaviors, with the expeditors doing whatever was needed to obtain the necessary SKU, sometimes by a process known as "strategic reallocation of resources"—or stealing, as one of the team put it!

The next step was to follow the guidelines for the development of the composite cloud, and this was soon completed. The cloud as developed is shown in Figure 4.4.

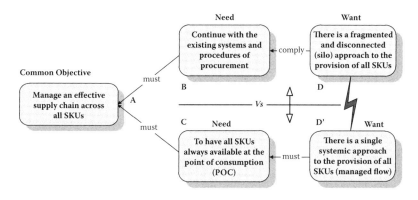

FIGURE 4.4
First MRO case study—composite cloud.

In reading this cloud, we can determine the nature of many of the behaviors within this particular MRO facility: "**In order to** *manage an effective supply chain across all SKUs* **we must** *have all SKUs always available at the point of consumption,* and **in order to** *have all SKUs available at the point of consumption* **there must** *be a single, systemic approach to the provision of all SKUs (managed flow).* However, **in order to** *manage an effective supply chain across all SKUs* **we must** *continue with the existing systems and procedures of procurement* **and in complying** *with those systems, there is a fragmented and disconnected (silo) approach to the provision of all SKUs.*"

At this point, I invited the team to consider what this analysis told them in terms of their ability to lead the MRO facility and what message needed to be sent throughout the supply chain in order to resolve the situation. The conflict between the silo mentality and the systemic one was clear to the whole team. They recognized, as did the leader of the team, that if this remained unresolved the situation would not improve, would in fact become more and more unmanageable, and probably lead to even more problems in the future. The devastating impact of the cross-connection was now clear, the dominant way of working—in silos—was central to the measurement system used by the corporate body, but the local impact at the point of consumption was disastrous. At the same time, even after there was agreement that a single, systemic approach might well be the right option—the right choice—the dominant measurement system would prevent such an idea gaining ground.

They were now invited to construct the CCRT (see Figure 4.5) and, once they had done so, to validate it through the use of the CLRs. The CCRT has great value in the communication of the analysis as it lends itself to being written as a report. The construction follows the rules for a Current Reality Tree (CRT). The CCRT for this case study is read in the following manner: if we want to manage an effective supply chain across all SKUs and if this is a core function of any supply chain, then we must have all SKUs, always available at the point of consumption. If we want to have all SKUs available at the point of consumption and if this represents a Lean supply chain then there is a single systemic approach to the provision of all SKUs (managed flow).

The importance of the "Lean supply chain" came from a corporate need to implement such an approach and then be able to show the merits of the approach to prospective clients; their argument was that this was the way to manage any MRO facility. Therefore the driver for the use of what the corporate function called Lean was to demonstrate world-class levels of

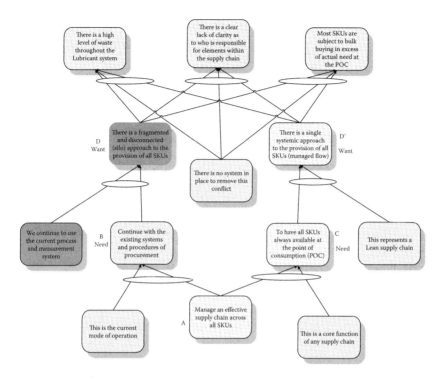

FIGURE 4.5
First MRO case study—CCRT.

performance within the whole of their supply chain. It was also noted by the team just how far away from any world-class measure of performance they were when the research project was completed. So, continuing with the reading, if we want to manage an effective supply chain across all SKUs and if this is our current mode of operation, we must continue with the existing systems and procedures of procurement. If we continue with our existing systems and procedures of procurement and if we continue with the current process and measurement system then there is a fragmented and disconnected (silo) approach to the provision of all SKUs. If we currently have this fragmented and disconnected approach to the provision of all SKUs, and if we want to have a single systemic approach to the same provision, and if there is no system in place to remove this conflict, then the other UDEs will also continue to exist, these being "there is a high level of waste throughout the lubricant system"; "there is a clear lack of clarity as to who is responsible for elements within the supply chain"; and "most SKUs are subject to bulk buying in excess of actual need at the POC." The team considered the analysis, checked it, and then communicated it to those throughout the organization who needed to see it, and who hopefully would respond to it. So at this point, we have arrived at the end of Station 2: we know what is holding us back and why. The next stage is to develop the compelling picture going forward, closing the performance gap, but this requires some key questions to be answered.

So now for the tricky bit! Put yourself in the position of the team leader. What choices do you have? What might you do having arrived at this conclusion? What would you do as the supply chain team leader, or perhaps the supply manager or director? What if you were the client that the MRO facility was supplying—how would you feel about this situation? What questions would you want to ask, what choices do you think you have, and what degrees of freedom to make those choices do you think you have? From the analysis above and in particular the DEs within each of the clouds, can you begin to paint a compelling picture? In each of the case studies, we had more UDEs than were used in the analysis. However, we did use all of the UDEs to determine the set of DEs which then formed part of the building blocks of the compelling picture. This picture was created using the Future Reality Tree (FRT) process with the key changes required to deliver the DEs included.

CASE STUDY 2 FROM AN MRO ENVIRONMENT

This second case study, also from an MRO environment, picks up a very different aspect. Indeed, what was interesting from the perspective of both case studies is that although from different environments, they had very similar ways of doing things. When I examined other MRO facilities engaged in very different products, I found the same issues time and time again, so in one sense I am content that the case studies described here are truly representative of many MRO facilities. This second case study started with an examination of a repair cell within the MRO facility and how it was able to meet the demands of the whole system. They were engaged in the repair of key components which formed a subassembly and which, when completed, enabled the primary unit to be reassembled and put back into service. The usual process of mapping was undertaken followed by the capturing of the UDEs from the people working in the repair cell, placing them into their respective locations on the map, trying to quantify the UDEs with respect to both financial and operational impact, writing and then reading the storylines, and checking back with the people concerned until we had a definitive UDE list. The first UDE was "**Key spares are not readily available at the point of consumption.**" This then led to the creation of the cloud shown in Figure 4.6.

Read in the usual manner, "**In order to** *have the repair bay meet all targets (on-time, in-full, right first time, return to service)* **we must have** *Fast Turn Around Time (TAT) within the bay* **because** *this ensures that the bay does not hold up the primary maintenance,* **because** *this reduces the level of WIP within the bay,* **because** *this gives us a high level of efficiency and effectiveness within the bay,* **because** *this represents a Lean environment.* **In order to** *have a Fast TAT within the bay* **we must have** *key spares available at the Point of Consumption (POC)* **because** *this ensures that resources operate at their most effective and efficient,* **because** *this ensures that all sub-assemblies are returned fit for purpose.* However, **in order to** *have the repair bay meet all targets,* **we must comply** *with the*

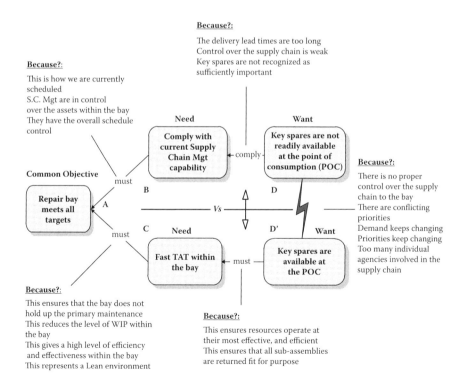

FIGURE 4.6

Second MRO case study UDE cloud 1.

current supply chain management capability, **because** *this is how we are currently scheduled,* **because** *the supply chain team control all the assets within the bay,* **because** *they, (supply chain mgt) have the overall schedule control.* **In complying with** *the current supply chain management capability* **we must manage** *the bay with key spares not readily available at the point of consumption (POC)* **because** *the delivery times are too long,* **because** *the control over the supply chain is weak,* **because** *key spares are not recognized as sufficiently important."* The statement written in the D box is in conflict with that written in the D' box "**because** *there are no proper controls over the supply chain to the bay,* **because** *there are conflicting priorities,* **because** *demands keeps changing,* **because** *priorities keep changing,* **because** *too many individual agencies are involved in the supply chain."*

Once more the same process of validation, checking the wording with the team, making sure that all the assumptions had been taken down correctly, and making any changes as necessary, was followed. The cross-connection was also examined and the impact was both clear and dramatic. In this case, the whole operational dimension of the bay was compromised due to the lack of spares being available as and when required. This led to a number of dysfunctional behaviors, such as taking some components off other subassemblies—stealing—in order to keep the flow going in the hope that the spares for the first item would arrive before the second was worked on.

Now the second UDE from the repair bay: "**There is a high backlog of components awaiting completion.**" The UDE cloud is shown below (see Figure 4.7) and reads in the normal manner. "**In order for** *the repair bay to meet all targets,* **there must** *be Fast TAT within the bay* **because** *this ensures the bay does not hold up the primary maintenance,* **because** *this reduces the level of WIP within the bay,* **because** *this gives a high level of efficiency and effectiveness within the bay,* **because** *this represents a Lean environment.* **In order to** *have Fast TAT within the bay* **there must** *be few components awaiting completion* **because** *(this way) we are able to complete each unit as soon as possible.* However, **in order to** *have the repair bay meet all targets* **we must comply** *with the current supply chain management capability,* **because** *this is how we are currently scheduled,* **because** *Supply Chain Management (SCM) are in control over the assets in the bay,* **because** *they (SCM) have the overall schedule control.* **In complying** *with the current supply chain mgt capability* **we must accept** *a high backlog of components awaiting completion*

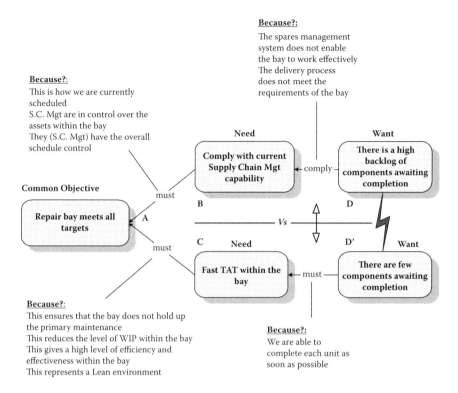

Because?:
The spares management
system does not enable
the bay to work effectively
The delivery process
does not meet the
requirements of the bay

Because?:
This is how we are currently
scheduled
S.C. Mgt are in control over the
assets within the bay
They (S.C. Mgt) have the overall
schedule control

Common Objective

Repair bay meets all
targets

must

A

Need

Comply with current
Supply Chain Mgt
capability

B

← comply

Want

There is a high
backlog of
components awaiting
completion

D

Vs

C   **Need**

Fast TAT within the
bay

← must →

D'   **Want**

There are few
components awaiting
completion

must

Because?:
This ensures that the bay does not hold up
the primary maintenance
This reduces the level of WIP within the bay
This gives a high level of efficiency and
effectiveness within the bay
This represents a Lean environment

Because?:
We are able to
complete each unit as
soon as possible

FIGURE 4.7
Second MRO case study UDE cloud 2.

because *the spares management system does not enable to bay to work effectively*, **because** *the delivery process (of spares) does not meet the requirements of the bay.*"

Once more the usual practice of checking the cloud was completed, and in the evaluation of the cross-connection many comments were made about the impact this had on the daily load. Often workers would only start on subassemblies that had a full set of spares and components; those that did not, even if they had a higher priority, were left to wait. If the priority was so high that something had to be done, then the old methods of seeking the component you needed, even if it was already on something else, and then using that (stealing), would happen. At the same time, there was pressure to buy more of the subassemblies in order to keep the final assembly bay working and thus returning equipment back to the primary user. It was pointed out that the cost of purchasing these new subassemblies was not cheap, and was much more than the cost of the missing items.

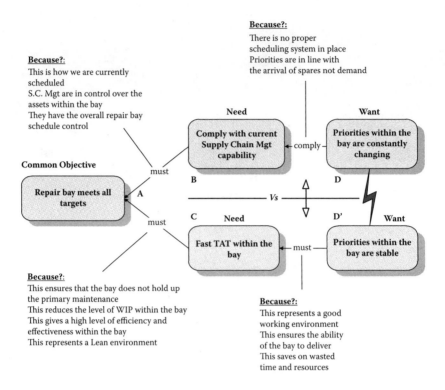

Because?:
There is no proper
scheduling system in place
Priorities are in line with
the arrival of spares not demand

Because?:
This is how we are currently
scheduled
S.C. Mgt are in control over the
assets within the bay
They have the overall repair bay
schedule control

Need

Want

**Comply with current
Supply Chain Mgt
capability** ←comply— **Priorities within the
bay are constantly
changing**

Common Objective

must

B

D

**Repair bay meets all
targets** A

Vs

must

C **Need**

D' **Want**

**Fast TAT within the
bay** —must— **Priorities within the
bay are stable**

Because?:
This ensures that the bay does not hold up
the primary maintenance
This reduces the level of WIP within the bay
This gives a high level of efficiency and
effectiveness within the bay
This represents a Lean environment

Because?:
This represents a good
working environment
This ensures the ability
of the bay to deliver
This saves on wasted
time and resources

FIGURE 4.8
Second MRO case study UDE cloud 3.

The choice of the final UDE was not a surprise: **Priorities within the bay are constantly changing** and the cloud was constructed in the time-honored manner as shown in Figure 4.8.

Again reading the cloud reveals the pressures that many people were experiencing within the bay. "**In order to** *have the repair bay meet all targets* **there must be** *fast TAT within the bay* for the same reasons as before. And **in order** *to have fast TAT within the bay* **we must have** *stable priorities within the bay* **because** *this represents a good working environment,* **because** *this ensures the ability of the bay to deliver,* **because** *this saves on wasted time and resources.* However, **in order to** *have the repair bay meet all targets* **we must comply** *with the current supply chain management capability* again for the same assumptions as before. **In complying with** *the current Supply Chain Management capability* **those within the repair bay must** *continue with the constantly changing priorities* **because** *there is no proper scheduling system in place,* **because** *the priorities are in line with the arrival of spares, not demand.*" Once again more validation took place, and the impact of the cross-connection formed part of a significant

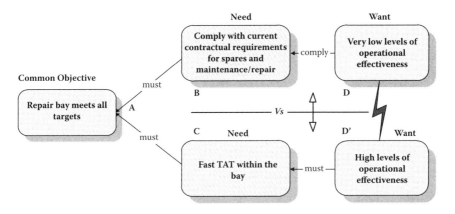

FIGURE 4.9
Second MRO case study—composite cloud.

discussion that took place, going into the issues that the recognition of this cross-connection offered. They were then invited to create the composite cloud using the usual process and this is shown in Figure 4.9.

The composite conflict resonated with all the team. The high levels of operational effectiveness that they sought—and indeed were required to achieve—were at odds with the current reality of extremely low levels of operational effectiveness. They knew this. They lived this conflict every day of their lives not just in the bay but throughout the whole of the MRO facility. But how to break free, that was a key question. Again, as with the other case studies they wanted to develop the ability to communicate this analysis, and so the CCRT shown in Figure 4.10 was developed and checked. The potential outcomes, coupled with the existing UDEs, showed clearly that something would have to change.

At this point we are once more at the completion of Stations 1 and 2 and ready for the next step in the cycle. Again, from the analyses here it is possible to determine the DEs and begin to flesh out a compelling picture, to encourage people within the team and the wider organization to add comments and question the analysis in readiness for closing the performance gap. So you are the bay leader—what choices do you have? You are the MRO manager—what choices do you have? You are the client of the MRO facility—what choices do you have? Just as with the first case study, what degrees of freedom do you have? Does the range of choices you have before you mandate different decisions? These questions were all faced by the bay manager, and his team, but what are your conclusions?

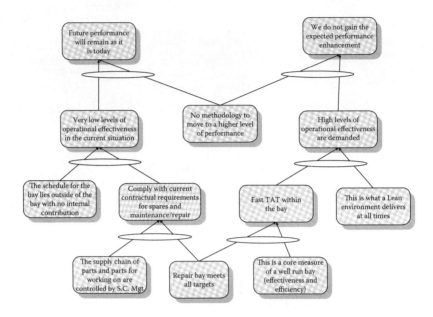

FIGURE 4.10
Second MRO case study—CCRT.

CASE STUDY 3 FROM AN OUTPATIENT DEPARTMENT IN A HOSPITAL

This case study, drawn from a completely different environment, was created following a series of meetings with the key staff of the outpatient department within a major hospital in the United Kingdom. The meetings comprised people from most aspects of patient care within the hospital including nursing staff, consultants, and administration. Each meeting followed a similar pattern, starting with an understanding of the way in which flow affected the people concerned, whether it be the flow of patients, of information, or some other form of flow; the importance of understanding the flow from the perspective of the individual was paramount.

Once the flow had been established, the next step was to ask for any problems and issues that surfaced on a regular basis. They are drawn from the area of responsibility of each person, and they are defined as being disturbing and at the same time on-going issues, therefore something that needed to be addressed in order to improve the level of service provided.

So the characteristics used to determine the UDEs in this case study were as follows:

1. The chosen issues are those that irritate you the most.
2. The chosen issues have a negative influence on your ability as a manager/leader within the organization to achieve your goals and those of your department or function.
3. The chosen issues exist frequently.

It is important that the issues chosen are stated in such a way that no one is blamed for the existence of the issues. This was checked through the validation of the both the UDEs and the storylines. Although many more than those listed were captured during the process of data collection, the statements listed in Figure 4.11 offer a clear and comprehensive description of what was presented and discussed.

In order to achieve a better understanding of the issues on hand it was then essential to understand the impact of all these problems and issues, the consequences of such issues on the individual, the team, and the organization as a whole. So I asked the question of one of the senior divisional managers within the hospital: What needs are being jeopardized by the

The UDEs from the Hospital

- *There is lack of prioritization in work being carried out*
- *There are conflicting roles and responsibilities at many levels*
- *There are conflicting targets and measurements (between departments and also within departments)*
- *There are no (few) standard operating procedures in many areas of work*
- *There are constant interruptions with requests for information not under our control*
- *There is a constant level of multi-tasking (taking time and effort away from critical tasks)*
- *There are no clear objectives in the daily work content*
- *There is constant rework activity in many different areas*
- *Work is passed to (our) area which has not been properly completed in the preceding area*
- *We (appointments) are under pressure to overbook the available capacity*
- *The real level of capacity available for patients is not known*

FIGURE 4.11
The UDEs from the hospital.

existence of these issues? Or in other words, which one of your needs as a manager do you feel you are unable to fully achieve because of the existence of these issues? These are her responses:

Fast flow of patients into and through the system. This is always at risk—they often enter quickly, but do not leave the system as quickly as they might expect.

Reducing the levels of delays. Patients often experience delays and changes to scheduled appointments—there is constant rescheduling of appointments, primarily follow-ups.

The sense of having done a good job for both the patients and the hospital. This is at risk.

Good staff morale and well-being. There are high levels of stress across departments—staff on long-term sickness is but one example of this.

Compliance with national measures and procedures. Patient pathways are not always complied with—if known to begin with.

This led to the next set of questions whereby the consequences can be more clearly determined. What action(s) are you forced to make to deal with the problems and issues these create in order to improve your ability to achieve the needs of the organization?

Constant rescheduling of patients after they have been allocated an outpatient appointment forces considerable effort in contacting patients and ensuring that the new appointment is suitable —often it is not.

Using additional resources in order to bring the timescales back into the targets we are required to achieve—this might involve additional nursing staff, additional clinics, etc.

Having resources available just in case even when not required, or not having them available and finding that they need to come in to meet unexpected demand.

Cancelling clinics.

Staff are constantly asked to change priorities of their work—urgent always take precedence over important.

Which one of your other needs, as a manager, prevents you from regularly taking the above action?

Targets make cancelling clinics impossible—yet still done.

Other clients such as the Primary Care Trust (PCT) or the Department of Health (DOH) require compliance with measurements—and often force appointments even when no capacity is available to enable them to take place.

Consultants often do not want to have their work disturbed or see any change to their work practices.

The primary need is to release new patients into the system rather than see existing patients leave the system.

Lack of authority over other parts of the hospital which directly affect my work and my ability to meet internal or external targets and measurements.

So moving from UDE to cloud (see Figure 4.12) we read:

UDE cloud 1: **there is constant re-work in many areas.** This UDE is taken from the scheduling department for the clinics, and the rework in question was the daily, constant rescheduling of appointments for patients, not any work being carried out on a patient. The cloud construction followed the usual pattern and is read in the following manner: **"In order to** *have fast flow of patients through the whole system* **we**

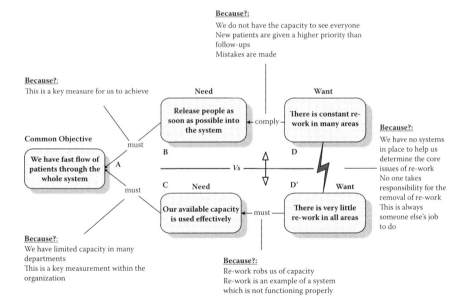

FIGURE 4.12
First UDE cloud from the hospital.

must have *our available capacity used effectively"* and **"In order to** *have our available capacity used effectively* **there must be** *little rework in all areas."* However, **"in order to have** *fast flow of patients through the whole system* **we must comply with** *the requirement to release new patients into the system as soon as possible,* and **in complying with** *the release of new patients as soon as possible* **we have** *constant re-work in many areas."* The assumptions that we have placed into the cloud are typical of those collected as part of this research study and symptomatic of the organization as a whole. As before, in order to understand the real impact of this conflict, it is useful to consider the cross-connection, the impact of the statement in the D' box to that of the B box, and then that of the D box on the C box. In this example, the impact of the D box to C is substantial; the constant rework clearly threatens the ability to use the available capacity effectively and thus the ability of the organization as a whole to achieve fast flow of patients through the whole system. So now we turn to UDE 2—(see Figure 4.13) many targets and measurements (within the organization) conflict (with each other).

This cloud is read in the same way as the preceding cloud. **"In order for** *us to be an effective organization to all our clients,* **we must have** *alignment of decisions throughout the organization (both sites).* **In order to have** *alignment of decisions throughout the organization* **we must have** *aligned targets and measurements.* However, **in order to** *be an effective organization to all our clients,* **we must comply** *with more than one governing body (PCT and DOH)* and **in complying with** *more than one governing body* **we have to** *work with many targets and measurements that are in conflict."* Again the cross-connection adds clarity to the real impact of this conflict. The impact of the D box containing the statement about the differing targets and measurements which are in conflict clearly affects the ability of those within the organization to align decisions throughout the whole. The assumptions are drawn from the data collected as part of the study. It is of interest to note that when I spoke at a Health Finance Managers Conference (April 2007) in Harrogate (United Kingdom) with a colleague, Steve Wray, this UDE dominated the session we were presenting on the application of Throughput Accounting. This UDE is rather commonplace throughout the National Health Service in the United Kingdom.

UDE cloud 3: **there is a lack of prioritization in work being carried out.** This is the third cloud drawn from the UDE list (see Figure 4.14). In this case the reading is as follows: **"in order to** *achieve the targets set for us*

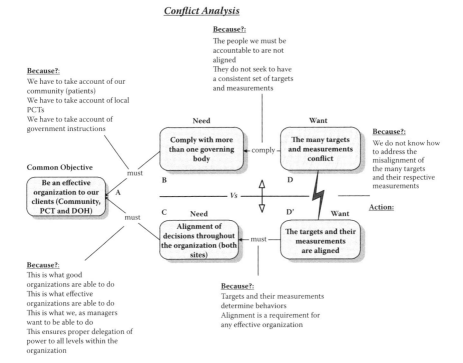

FIGURE 4.13

Second UDE cloud from the hospital.

as a hospital (global) **we must** *operate the hospital as a systemic organization,* and **in order to** *operate the hospital in this way* **there must be** *clear prioritization in the work being carried out.* However, **in order to** *achieve the targets set for us as a hospital,* **we must comply with** *the current practice of managing the hospital as a series of discrete and independent entities,* and **in complying** *with this approach there is a lack of prioritization in the work being carried out.*"

This time the cross-connection works in both directions. The D box aggravates the ability to operate the hospital as a systemic organization with clear dependencies on functions throughout the system as a whole, and the D' box affects the current mode of operation, which is to manage the system as if they are discrete entities with limited dependency between them.

So what happens when we move to the construction of the composite cloud? The next step is to develop the three clouds as constructed into one single and coherent cloud which encapsulates the three and yet gives a

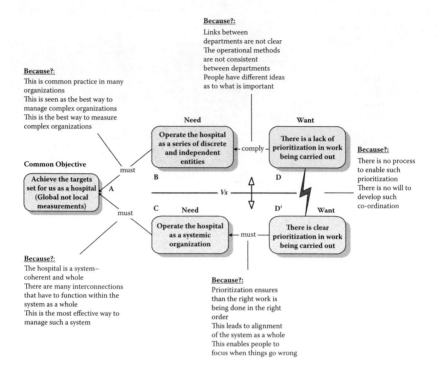

Because?:
Links between
departments are not clear
The operational methods
are not consistent
between departments
People have different ideas
as to what is important

Because?:
This is common practice in many
organizations
This is seen as the best way to
manage complex organizations
This is the best way to measure
complex organizations

Need
B | Operate the hospital
as a series of discrete
and independent
entities | ←comply→ | **Want**
There is a lack of
prioritization in work
being carried out

Because?:
There is no process
to enable such
prioritization
There is no will to
develop such
co-ordination

Common Objective
Achieve the targets
set for us as a hospital
(Global not local
measurements) | A

must

— Vs —

D

must

C Need
Operate the hospital
as a systemic
organization | ← must — | **D' Want**
There is clear
prioritization in work
being carried out

Because?:
The hospital is a system—
coherent and whole
There are many interconnections
that have to function within the
system as a whole
This is the most effective way to
manage such a system

Because?:
Prioritization ensures
than the right work is
being done in the right
order
This leads to alignment
of the system as a whole
This enables people to
focus when things go wrong

FIGURE 4.14
Third UDE cloud from the hospital.

deeper insight as to the problems and issues affecting the organization as a whole (see Figure 4.15).

Once constructed, this composite cloud can be read in the usual manner. "**In order to** *fully satisfy the needs of our clients (PCT, Community, and DOH)* **we must be** *able to achieve high levels of patient flow through the whole system.* **In order to achieve high levels of patient flow through the whole system** *our (future) current mode of operation* **must be** *fully aligned in terms of consistency of purpose and systemic understanding.*

"However, **in order to** *fully satisfy the needs of our clients (PCT, Community, and DOH)* **we must comply** *with the current individual needs of each department and each client in terms of their own targets and measurements* and **in complying with this,** *our current mode of operation is fragmented in terms of alignment, consistency of purpose, and systemic understanding.*"

The conclusion the team came to was that this represented the core conflict within hospital based on the data collected. Once more the use of the cross-connection shows the devastating impact of the conflict. The

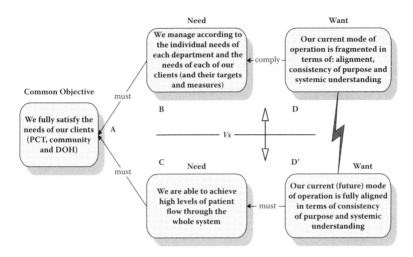

FIGURE 4.15
Composite cloud from the hospital.

current fragmented mode of operation dealt a major blow to the need for fast patient flow through the whole of the system, and the desired mode of operation can be seen as threatening current expectations and individual preferences for each department or client. The dysfunctional behaviors, the high levels of stress within key members of staff, were all seen as indicative of the system as it was currently being run. The need for changing the primary methods of managing the organization was laid bare. The need for clear communication of this analysis and the conclusions drawn from it still required careful presentation.

We can now construct the logical analysis, the CCRT, that shows the pressures that existed within the hospital at present time (see Figure 4.16).

This analysis is read in the following manner starting at the bottom. "**If** *we want to fully satisfy the needs of our clients* **and if** *a key measure of satisfaction to all our clients (internal and external) is a reduction in waiting time,* **then** *we want to be able to achieve high levels of patient flow through the whole system.* **If** *we want to be able to achieve high levels of patient flow through the whole system* **and if** *patient flow is dependent on an aligned and synchronized system,* **then** *we are under pressure to change our current mode of operation to one that is fully aligned in terms of consistency of purpose and systemic understanding.*" The other side of the analysis would then be read in the same way.

We can now ask a simple question, given this logical analysis: Can we see any connection between it and the remaining UDEs not used to construct

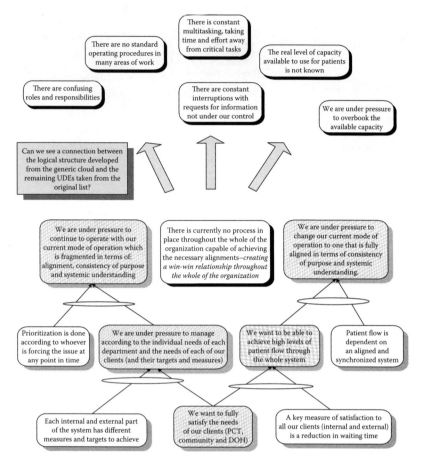

FIGURE 4.16
CCRT from the hospital.

the clouds? If the answer is yes then, as before with our case studies, we have been able to determine the answer to the first question "What to change?" which is contained in the statement, "There is currently no process in place throughout the whole of the organization capable of achieving the necessary alignments—thus creating a win-win set of relationships throughout the whole of the organization." At this point, Stations 1 and 2 of the coaching cycle have been completed and we are ready to consider the choices that lie before us and then the creation of the compelling picture going forward. As before the same questions apply, what are our choices? What degrees of freedom do we have?

In order to reinforce this analysis, what follows is a simple logical structure of an incident that took place during the research process and demonstrates the issues clearly. It is, in fact, an example of another tool within the TP toolset, that of a Negative Branch Reservation or NBR. The analysis is read in the same way as before, but note the loop which leaves the statement at the top and returns to one further down the logical structure—entering at the statement, "The task of carrying out the changes comes to people working in appointments." The impact of this loop is to make matters even worse than before, and this is a continual fact of life within the department concerned.

I captured this example as I stood in the room where the appointments were made. The driver for the sequence of events that I witnessed started with the statement "Consultant requires one more patient to be added to the list for next week and four to be removed." Seems a simple enough request, but what followed was both fascinating and disturbing. The process of changing the appointments was followed. The staff in the office concerned found themselves, as they usually do, in the situation of having to make decisions entirely based on the decisions made by the consultant, made for good reasons I have no doubt, but which now had an impact that the consultant never saw. In this case, more than twenty-two people had to be moved, and this is only one incident, involving one consultant, and there are many more in the hospital, all seeking the same level of service from the booking team. Everyone agreed there had to be a better way, but no one seemed to know where to start, or even if they were allowed to question the current rules and procedures (see Figure 4.17).

We have now examined the three case studies partway through the coaching cycle. We have mapped the process from the start. We have captured UDEs from those involved in the process and placed them on the map. In some cases, we will have determined the financial cost of the UDE and in all cases determined the impact of the full set of UDEs on the goal and necessary conditions. We have used the UDEs to construct the individual clouds, surface assumptions, and then build the composite cloud. From that we proceeded to the CCRT and used that to check whether the UDEs not used still connect. We have been able to list the DEs that a solution would be expected to deliver and have begun to think of the changes that must be completed for the DEs to be achieved. We have communicated both the CCRT and, in outline at the very least, the compelling picture to as wide an audience as possible. Now we have choices to make. What is the best way forward? What does the full solution consist of? How do I/we gain the engagement of the rest of the team? How do I lead the team forward from this point? These are some of the key questions an effective leader has now to deal with. We will return to the case studies in Chapter 7, but before we do I want to examine leadership in the context of the team and that of the leader him- or herself.

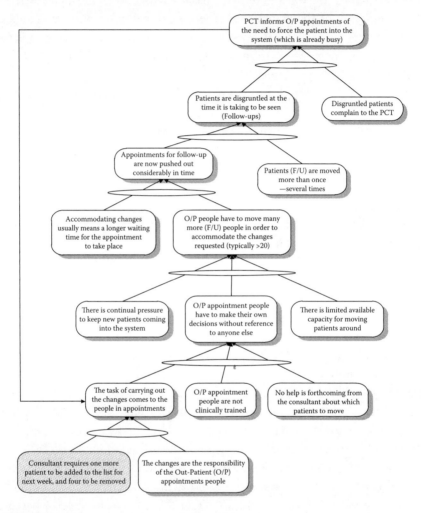

FIGURE 4.17
A final thought about consequences.

5

Leading the Team

UNDERSTANDING THE DYNAMICS
OF TEAM LEADERSHIP

It is interesting that in the past twenty years of working with a wide range of organizations, throughout the United Kingdom and Europe, the United States, Australia and New Zealand, just how many times I came across people very busily trying to improve the performance of their organization yet when pressed they could not state with any confidence what the goal of the business was. This applied to all the sectors I worked with— private, public, service, and voluntary. Of course, some people are very busy and almost all were citing the need for more people, more orders, more money, more this and that, but all this without any real conviction as to what the goal was, other than some esoteric notion of what the business might be about. In some cases, there was only a heavy dependence on efficiency measures, "as long as we are busy, nothing else matters" as one senior manager said to me. In November 2007, I attended the ProjectWorld conference in Philadelphia where the main speaker was Stephen Covey. He asked us all to close our eyes and point north, then, keeping our arms pointing north, to open our eyes and look around. As you might imagine, there were people pointing in all directions, and his lesson was simple: if the goal is to go north, and you have no idea where north is, then working as hard and as fast as you can in the wrong direction remains the wrong direction. Busy you will be, thus you will be efficient, but effective—no. So, as already noted, the ability to define the goal and the necessary conditions is a critical starting point. From this clarity, it is possible to define the goal units, which will help us with the creation of good measurements. Only now are we in a position to communicate just what the goal is to everyone in the organization and beyond. We can also communicate what the necessary conditions are, and make sure that everyone knows what their unique contribution is to both.

LEADING THE TEAM TO ACHIEVE THE GOAL

In each of the case studies described in this book the leader was working through a team. The membership of the team was not always constant. Some people moved in, others moved out, and of course some stayed. This was, more often than not, simply recognizing that for some projects the individual team members might have to change in order to include specialist knowledge or some other skill deemed important by the leader and the other team members. In this chapter, I want to explore what was going on within the teams involved in each of the case studies, what issues were being surfaced as a result of working together on these organizational problems, and how the team responded, both as a collective and/or as an individual team member. I will also describe some ways forward that we developed in order to improve the ability of both the leader and the team.

In the context of those who took part in the data capture, the importance of the team to those taking part in the research was both dominant, and a key source of worry. After discussions with a variety of people drawn from both the companies involved in the case studies and from other sectors, such as voluntary (e.g., the Church of England), both in their roles as leaders and as members of teams, six key aspects were identified that those involved felt led to the creation of successful teams.

1. **Making good team choices**: This was primarily focused on the added dimension that team members would undoubtedly bring to the problems being addressed. This ability to make good team choices was recognized as a function of the problem definition process as described in Station 2 of the coaching cycle, but knowing the core problem does not always mean that the way forward is equally clear. There will be choices that need to be made. However, what is a good choice for one member might not be so for another! Division is to be expected. But

the leader helps each team member to put aside their own individual objectives and subordinate to those of the organization as a whole—this is collective responsibility. This requires everyone to focus on the same goal and understand the necessary conditions; this is consensus. And then there are a whole host of other questions that need to be answered. What is the context of the choice? Can we fully describe the choices that lie before us? Do we all have the same understanding, the same knowledge of these choices? Are they clear? Do we know the assumptions that lie behind each choice, and if so do we know them with sufficient clarity? Do we agree with the assumptions? Are there some missing? Are some erroneous? Just how do the choices before us relate to our team goals, objectives, and necessary conditions? Of course, the ability to answer these questions with some level of confidence lies in the robustness of the analysis of the current problems and issues facing the team. When the importance of making sound choices shifts from the leader to the team, the robustness of the analysis, this time carried out as a team rather than just the leader doing it and inviting the team members to comment, becomes central. How have the choices been determined? Was the rigor of the coaching cycle used to ensure proper focus throughout the team and throughout the process of analysis? In terms of all the case studies used, this point was achieved at the end of Station 3—painting the compelling picture—having already defined to the satisfaction of all the team members the core problem and why it exists. This can now be accepted as the central aspect of preparation for moving to Station 4—achieving the objectives set.

2. **Making good team decisions:** This followed the same path as before with respect to choices. For each of the possible choices that faced the team there are a set of decisions that follow the choice. The questions about the links between choices and the decisions that follow the choice need to be properly answered, and this involves knowing the definition of each decision. Indeed, can it be defined with sufficient clarity to enable the necessary communication that must take place to the rest of the organization? Just what are the decisions that need to be taken and what actions do they contain? Can we communicate the decisions to each team member, and then to those outside the team, including those affected directly and those peripherally affected, and in some cases to those not affected at all?

3. **The ability to delegate effectively:** This opened up the whole area of team building, team membership, team roles, team psychology, and the importance of intrateam communication. It also involved developing the ability to resolve internal team conflicts as a win-win; resolving any delegation issues and working out rules and procedures that delivered, rather than prevented, the end result, the desired outcomes. Did the members of the team feel they had the necessary authority to carry out the actions being delegated? Did they feel they owned what was being delegated? Did they have any flexibility over the actions, and could they change them if they appeared not to be leading the organization forward? This is where the leader can have huge impact. If he or she retains some of this authority, then the other members of the team feel as if they are not being trusted, and if the leader gives away all of the authority—what happens when it goes wrong? Will they be held responsible for the actions of their team?

4. **Understanding consequences**: This returned to much the same issues as above, but of course with the added complication of more than one person suggesting potential negative outcomes, thus making the process more complex, and the possibility of conflict higher. The same desires dominated, however; can we identify the potential negatives—and if so—what can we do about them, and can we develop solutions to these outcomes before they affect what we are trying to achieve? It is interesting to note that positive outcomes and consequences were not of great interest other than to help in the buy-in process with the rest of the organization. Riding roughshod over these potential negatives was also highly counterproductive. When this happened, the rest of the team typically gave up offering such observations, preferring to let the leader find them out for him- or herself.

5. **Resolving conflicts within the team:** This was a critical area to address as most people recognized that such conflicts were an almost daily occurrence, and they recognized the damaging effect they usually had. If any situation best defined the issues of broken relationships within the team, and indeed beyond into the rest of the organization, it was this area of unresolved conflicts. This applied, in particular, to those conflicts that had been allowed to remain unresolved for some time and had thus become open sores within the team, with all the inevitable consequences. Many times conflicts were dealt with by

force rather than reason, by gaining submission but not resolution. This often meant that there was no sense of achieving win-win, but only a feeling that more trouble had been stored up storing for later on frequently with devastating results. The inability to surface the deep causality within all these conflicts meant that those involved were highly likely to be doomed to repeat the pain again and again.

6. **Resolving conflicts between teams**: Once the conflict within the team was recognized, the impact on other teams, both within the rest of the organization and beyond to teams that lay outside, was also recognized. The pattern of broken relationships extended way beyond the immediate vicinity of the original team, and it had the capacity to poison relationships in all manner of ways that could not be identified without the focusing power of the analysis. This too was felt to be a vital part of developing a sound platform for the ongoing growth of the company without sacrificing stability of relationships.

MEASURING THE PROGRESS OF THE TEAM

Given that the team was being asked to address core issues within the organization and as part of that process to implement change while still doing the day job, measuring progress is clearly a vital dimension. Is the new approach defined by the problem analysis and the development of an implementable solution making progress, and are the other responsibilities that the members of the team all have also being taken care of? Whenever we are implementing a TOC-based solution, the core tools employed are the Prerequisite Tree (PRT) where the primary Intermediate Objectives (IO) are defined and structured in a logic and time dependency and the Transition Tree (TRT) where the actions required for each IO are also determined in a logic and time dependency structure. More on these can be found in the standard literature of the TOC, in particular that of Scheinkopf (1999). Once I have developed such an implementation plan, I typically convert it to a project plan and then use the Critical Chain Project Management (CCPM) to monitor progress, allocate the right people, and take the necessary actions in line with the plan. Thus I have a high level of confidence that all will come to completion on time, and in full, and to budget!

Recently a new and more dynamic approach has been developed called the Strategy and Tactics Tree (S&T). This again is a very powerful tool and is of greatest value in the communication of the proposed implementation, its core dimensions, and how it all fits into the overall strategy of the business, which is itself defined through the use of the S&T trees. Using these tools, it is relatively easy to measure progress, determine the points where it has stalled, and develop interventions that get the implementation project tasks back on track. So in terms of measurement, I can use the project plan, the progress within the context of the PRT and the TRT, and the S&T construct to help. The question of measurement does take us back to the common lack of clarity with respect to the goals and objectives being sought and necessary conditions to attain these, coupled with the need for suitable measures, which could be understood by all the team members. This is vital and should be noted right at the start. Thus the knowledge of where the team was at the start, clearly a requirement, is nevertheless often missing. Remember, given the constant drive for better performance, often without any real idea of the correct direction, such driving can only lead to greater, local, activity, and more often than not, little or no progress toward the overall goal.

MAKING IT HAPPEN

In terms of the ability to implement successfully I have found that the importance of the coaching cycle must be coupled with the development of the team to make it happen. I have found it to be of great value to first develop what I call the "flight crew." The second element that must happen is to work through five critical, strategic steps related to the change process, and finally to make full use of a simple idea known as the 4Ps.

The Flight Crew

So what is the flight crew? Think of the flight crew on board an aircraft taking you from London to Seattle. There is one overall team, with a leader. There are also teams within the team, one in the cockpit and another in the cabin. Each member of either team has a set of skills, some unique to them, some common to all the members. They each know their roles and

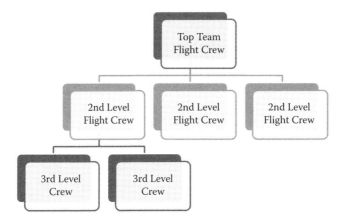

FIGURE 5.1
Basic flight crew structure.

responsibilities and how they are to work together on the journey to the goal—a safe landing in Seattle. I have found the idea of such a description for a team to be of great value. Others, notably Robin Gamble (2009), use the term "cockpit crew" in much the same way.

As is shown in Figure 5.1 there is an overall flight crew—this is level 1. Then below that is the second level and below that the third level. At least one member of the higher team will be in the next level down, so for example, from the Top Team Flight Crew at least one member will be in the second level and so on down through, and across, the organization.

Thus the flight crew is the core team of the leader at any level. In the context of organizational development, they will have been instrumental in the data collection process. They will have fully engaged with the analysis and the validation that follows. They will have communicated what is going on to their own team members, and to the wider people throughout the organization. They will have specialist knowledge of not just their function but also other aspects of value to the team and the leader. They might often be the leader of their own teams in the organization. Part of what they will be expected to do is to develop their own flight crews as the means by which they are able to engage with people at a lower level within the organization.

The flight crew, with the support and guidance of the leader, is central to the determination of the strategy of the organization. Often each member of the core flight crew will have their own flight crew and the teams within their own function will be responsible for the tactical implementation of the higher level strategy. This is one of the key areas in which the

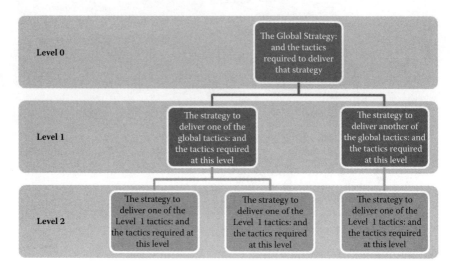

FIGURE 5.2
The basic strategy and tactics structure.

S&T approach pays real dividends, and I will map the flight crew model directly to that of the S&T (see Figure 5.2).

I often use the term DNA to help people understand this critical aspect. "D" stands for *determining the benefits,* which is where, in both the analysis and the communication, the desired outcomes are clearly defined and transmitted throughout the organization. This helps to reinforce the goals and necessary conditions while helping to raise potential negative outcomes and more obstacles to the proposed solutions. It is the point at which I am able to show both the direction of the solution and the expected benefits which must comprise a win-win for all parties. I use the combination of the S&T approach coupled with the FRT and PRT to help define this step in preparation for the communication. For "N," I mean ensuring that the *need for planning* has been fully accepted and the steps that have been used in the project planning process are understood. This works at both the macro level with the tools (again S&T, FRT, and PRT) contained within the TOC approach and also within the coaching cycle right down to the detail of the actions contained within the plan. Engaging with people at this stage rarely disappoints. They have great intuition about the possible problems and show-stoppers that lie in wait, and thus listening to their concerns always pays a high dividend. Finally "A" is for *actions,* those needed to implement the solution, make it work, make it happen. Here I use the Critical Chain Project Management Approach (CCPM). It is clearly not enough to plan the actions in time and logic dependency, but they must also be completed, so there is a need for measures that determine progress toward completion which is where buffer management makes such a vital contribution. Making it happen once all the analysis, all the planning, and all the communication has been completed seems, at least to me, the most obvious next step. Why it sometimes does not happen will be discussed in Chapter 7. However, there are times when things, in the execution of the plan, do not go according to the plan, when things stall or go off at an unexpected tangent. We have used the same tools as for the creation of the plan, coupled with the buffer management inherent in Critical Chain to address those issues. The ability to tap into what is happening, and the perceptions that exist, throughout the organization using the flight crew are never to be underestimated.

In my work both with the case studies drawn from manufacturing, MRO and NHS described earlier in this book and throughout industry I have noticed five key steps in any successful implementation or project execution.

1. The first is to establish positive leadership, starting with the leader and then the flight crew. This is critical for the successful outcome on any change program: if the leader fails to recognize the importance of actually leading, then the likelihood of failure is high.

2. The second is to become a mission/goal focused company as soon as possible, *ASAP.* This stands for *attitudes, strategies, activities,* and *personal leadership.* It is when people see these being promoted and practiced that they feel they can follow both the leader and the journey while at the same time feeling they have been involved in the process, able to contribute, challenge, think about the choices and decisions being made, and thus feel valued.

3. The third is to set up regular team briefings at all levels, starting with the flight crew. Indeed, I usually suggest that the flight crew make regular presentations to the senior management or even the board. The skill associated with giving such briefings has to be developed, but the investment rarely fails to deliver in terms of consistency and alignment of decision making and purpose.

4. The fourth is to create a real sense of community within the organization, focused on making it more effective in the chosen markets. I have seen such flight crews change where they work, moving to

be closer together, working around the same desk area with white-boards and flip charts in close attendance.

5. And finally, maintaining support at all levels to take the organization forward. It is all about communication and developing sound relationships throughout, repairing those that are broken and encouraging new and perhaps more innovative relationships to flourish in the future.

The fifth step makes mention of communication, and this is where we really concentrate on the communication of what is happening, what changes are taking place, and the impact these changes will have on the people and also the business. There is little value in leading an organization to have wonderful ideas, develop ground-breaking solutions, coupled with perfect project plans, if what is being done is never communicated, or communicated so badly that the only result is failure.

It starts with *Preparation*, which is where the leader prepares first and then invites the flight crew to do the same, and then they come together to develop the message, the narrative that will be used at all levels and for all to think, consider, and challenge. This will also lead to others within the organization helping with both the communication and the development of the implementation through raising more reservations than have already been noted. There is often a huge amount of data that can be used for the content of the narrative. The flight crew will have been at the center of the analysis; they will have had access to all the supporting data necessary to create a robust and exciting picture going forward, a compelling picture. They should test the message on themselves, seeking out the gaps in the narrative and the jumps in the logic that may prevent understanding being communicated.

The next step is *Promotion*, in which the leader and the flight crew make sure that everyone is on-board, the compelling picture going forward is understood, and any issues are captured and dealt with. This is not a one-off event; it is ongoing for some considerable time. People will forget the message; they will, under pressure, revert to the way things were done previously. There will be questions and misconceptions and misperceptions arising all the time. Hence there is a need to maintain the promotion well after the changes have been completed.

The next step is developing a real *Presence*, and this step demands great care and excellent execution. We need to make sure that the message is confirmed and everyone can see their contribution. Coaching, mentoring, and supporting are core activities here and should not be overlooked.

Finally there is *Persuasion*, in which it might well be necessary to sit beside someone who is having problems in understanding. This is best done one to one or in small-group work, and can be taken down from the top to the shop floor. This is often the place where external coaches can have a huge impact.

But what of the leader? Over the years, I have seen firsthand those who have the qualities to be good leaders either frozen out by those who are afraid of such people, or become so overloaded with day-to-day administration that they are never able to demonstrate what they might be able to do. At the same time, I have found myself spending more and more time simply listening to their story and the choices they have made, so perhaps now is the time to consider the role of the individual.

REFERENCES AND FURTHER READING

Gamble, R. *Jesus the Evangelist*. Eastbourne, UK: David C. Cook, 2009.
Scheinkopf, L. *Thinking for a Change*. Boca Raton, FL: St. Lucie Press, 1999.

6

Focusing on "Knowing Myself" as a Core Aspect of Leadership

THE LEGACY OF LEADERSHIP

So far I have spent some considerable time discussing leadership from a team or organizational perspective. The case studies are primarily about this, but what about the person who is the leader. What of their issues, their problems, their fears, their hopes, their aspirations? This is the time to consider the person at the center of all this, the leader him- or herself.

There are a number of questions that leaders need to answer for themselves, questions that help them to understand just who they are as people and from that how they might pick up the challenge of leadership. The first is simply "how well do I know myself?" Seems a simple enough question, but I have found many people who struggled to reach a satisfactory answer and therefore sought help to do so. Simon and Shaw (2011) consider in their introduction, "The most fundamental factor that affects our leadership is who we are: our values, our character, our attitudes and our personality" (p. xiii). So starting with this question is important. In this respect, I have used, over the years, many tools and techniques such as the Myers-Briggs Type Indicator and the Belbin approach. What is critical here is to use whatever methods seem appropriate and effective—the tool is less important than the information and insights it gives.

A second question is "how well do I manage my time, my priorities?" Once more, I have found that essential balance in life to be skewed often detrimentally especially with respect to relationships. Third, "how well do

97

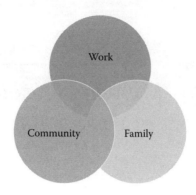

FIGURE 6.1
The three aspects of my life.

I know what I want to achieve as a leader?" With this question, the focus shifts from me as a person to my role as leader within the organization. The fourth question, "how well do I know and understand those trends both within and without the organization that need to be developed or countered?" examines my role and now continues with highlighting partly what leaders are supposed to do, looking for the threats and the opportunities facing the organization at any one point in time. This leads to the final question, which is "how well have I analyzed these threats and opportunities in order to lead the organization forward?"

Of course these questions need a context, and this is provided by returning to a continuing theme within this book, that of knowing both the goal of the organization and the necessary conditions in achieving it. This returns us to the importance of painting a compelling picture, having a vision as to where the organization can go, and translating it into a strategy that all within the organization can align with. Of course, it is of little importance for the leader to assume that everyone agrees to the goal, knows the necessary conditions, the strategy, and the tactics that will enable the achievement of all this, if it is not communicated clearly. The leader needs to communicate to everyone and then check that all understand what is being asked of them, the context in which that sits, the core measures that determine progress toward the goal. Do they own the goal? Do they own the strategy and the tactics required? Do they know how to communicate all this to their people in their teams, and if not, why not?

Knowing who I am allows me to begin the process of what being a leader is all about. Once I have understood this aspect I am able to set out on the journey, with confirmation from my team, taking the organization from where it is to where it needs to be. This is where I met many people for whom the ability to create a lasting legacy was very important. So, just as with an organization, knowing my goal in life and the relevant necessary conditions applies here as a core aspect of knowing myself.

This was particularly the case with many of those I met who were leading organizations; they saw their work very much in terms of legacy, a sense of what they hoped to leave behind after they had left, retired, or in some cases died. They saw this as part of a simple process: if they wanted to leave a legacy for their organization, then they had to do so for the team for which they were primarily responsible. This is the reason why they required a recognition, an understanding, of their own personal leadership style and how that impinged on their team and the organization.

So in terms of legacy, what were the common themes that people were struggling with? I soon identified five aspects that seemed to occupy the minds of those I was working with at the time.

1. **Making good choices**: Within this dimension, I found a number of key aspects that dominated their thinking. These were questions such as how do I define what a "good choice" is? What conditions the range of choices I have? How do I describe the choices that lie before me? Is it possible to surface the assumptions upon which I might make the choice? The notion of "choice" always seemed to lie in the area of life choices, or major strategic shifts within the organization or team. There was an implicit assumption that the choice was related to some idea of a goal—but such a thing was rarely defined too precisely! It is important here to remember what was discussed earlier in Chapter 1 about what is meant by the term "good choices." Returning to the theme and reminding ourselves of the core issues related to what constitutes a good choice is always valuable. Of course, during the data gathering that took place for the book I met some who felt that whatever they were trying to achieve was probably going to work even if they never made a choice—just let fate take the lead, go with the flow, and don't make waves. For some, the need to make a choice was also between two core drivers, fear or a problem that could not be avoided. If the fear level was low, they would wait until it was higher and then think about whether a choice was required or not. If it was problem-driven they might wait until someone else told them to do something about it, in which case it was often a combination of fear and the problem that drove the choice

making. There were times when making the choice was all about trying to achieve a goal, at other times it was to avoid a disaster, and then there were those choices that were in response to some form of compliance with higher authority.

2. **Making good decisions**: This followed naturally from the field of choices but brought with it issues, such as, can I recognize the decisions that each choice requires in order to be properly executed? Do I actually know what is meant by the term "good decision"? Can I communicate what I am trying to achieve to those around me? Do I understand the assumptions I am making, and can I communicate them to those around me? At the same time, most people I spoke to felt they were making decisions all the time, just not those that fitted the description "good."

3. **Understanding negative consequences:** This was fascinating, for most of those I worked with knew only too well the impact of negative consequences. However, more often than not, they chose to ignore the likely impact, assuming that it would all work out in the long run. This was a view that rarely did work out in practice, but was common nevertheless! Dominating their thinking were questions, such as, how might these consequences actually happen? How can I avoid what I think is going to happen? Can I see it before it hits me?

4. **Measuring progress:** Here the use of measurements became quite important, and at the same time came the discovery that many teams, and individuals, had no real measurement at all! This also started with the recognition that without a target, a description of the goal, measurement was unlikely to be of any value. So do I know the target? Do I actually know my goal in life? Can I measure progress toward where I want to be, and what are the units of measurement? Can I close the gap and do I actually know the starting point? Can I answer the question of where I am today?

5. **Obtaining balance:** If any one aspect was deemed to be of greatest importance, it was this one; yet at the same time, this was the area most compromised. This was where the three aspects that I have used within this book really came to the fore. How to develop the ability to balance work, home, and other relationships had become of supreme importance. Most knew that relationships in at least one area of their life were being put at risk, or were already broken, as a consequence of trying to achieve something in the dominant area of their life. The whole question of balance was something for "later,"

which usually meant "never"! I met many people who were struggling with all manner of things at home, struggling with all manner of pressures at work, and were using some other form of outlet, such golf, drinking, and socializing, not to mention a few others as well, in order to try and relieve the pressure they were under. I met many who had spent time off on stress-related sick leave, many who had cracked under the pressure, many who had experienced pain in terms of their family relationships, and still they continued to stay where they were.

There were also positives associated with obtaining balance: the importance of developing a sense of both individual and team greatness, even organizational greatness, was clear in many instances, as the alignment of goals, expectations, and outcomes became complementary rather than conflicting. When this level of congruence occurred, the impact on relationships at home and within the community in which they lived also improved dramatically.

USING "PERSONAL FOCUS" TO GAIN BALANCE

In Chapter 1, I described this three-circle diagram and the typical levels of imbalance I found with many of the people I have worked with. The imbalance comes from any one of the circles dominating the other two. The resulting level and impact of the dysfunctional relationships, broken relationships, stress related disorders, even broken marriages in some cases, ill health, pain, anger, frustration were clear. The list goes on and was both common and debilitating for those affected.

The question I asked myself back in 1996 was simply this: "Does it have to be this way?" To which I answered with an emphatic "No"! At the time, I did not really know how to address such a range of problems, but I did see them as a connected set of issues in a disconnected life. I knew of others active in this field at the time. People such as Limor Winter-Kraemer, Kathy Austin, Eliyahu Goldratt, Oded Cohen, and others were all using the 3-UDE cloud process to help, on a one-to-one basis, the person they were working with break free from these issues, should they choose to do so.

I began using the same process and continued to develop it not just in my professional work with clients from organizations large and small, but also, more recently, in the church where my role as spiritual director forms part of my current ministry. The starting point was for the person to recognize they needed help, akin to those who seek help from Alcoholics Anonymous. Help is not really forthcoming until you accept the need for it; you have to want it; it has to be a conscious choice or it simply does not work. So once they had accepted that they needed help, I would then sit down with them and start to write.

The stations of the coaching cycle provide the framework, working at the level of the individual. Most often I was asked to do this by people who knew I could help them. I would sit with them, asking them to tell me their story, listening carefully as they spoke, listening for the UDEs and the associated storylines. It is impossible to underestimate the importance of listening at this step. I am being told a story, and part of the discipline of listening is not to interrupt, not to offer a solution, not to try and tell my own story. If I am listening with both ears and eyes, I soon learn much more than the person I am working with intends. Much more is given away as to what is happening in their life than they imagine. Listening to their story is a privilege and one that demands total confidentiality and a sensitive compassion to the person and their story.

As I listened, I would write down what they were saying and every so often would take them through what I had written, giving a short summary rather than trying to feedback all that had been said. They would sometimes just nod in agreement; at other times they might suggest a change to the words I had used, but practice meant that most times what I had written really captured the story and the problems. There were also times when they would change what was written as they felt themselves had not really given sufficient clarity. The only questions I would ask at this point would be clarity questions where I myself did not understand what was being said. I was seeking to understand, perhaps inviting them to retell the story in order to seek what was lying behind the superficial level of the story. Slowly but surely I would start to capture a number of key points.

These key points would come at me in no particular order, but before long I would have a basic understanding of at least six or seven UDEs, and they would almost always come from the three dominant aspects of their life—home, work, and community. With those UDEs, I could then use my cloud template, in my notebook, to begin the process of writing the clouds. I would ask the questions that helped me to fill in each of the five boxes of the cloud structure and complete, slowly, gently and maybe over two or three sessions, three UDE clouds, one from work, one from home, and one from community. When I looked at the three clouds, before any feedback took place toward the person concerned, I was always struck, and still am, at the pressure some people were living with, the pain, the constant stress these conflicts must have been causing, and the impact they must have been having on many of their relationships.

So I would now have three clouds and a reasonable understanding of the predicament the person was in, plus the range of emotions they were experiencing. I would then be in a position to read each of the clouds, in turn, back to the person, taking each step slowly, checking for the right words, changing any words that the person had a problem with or wished to substitute with a word that was clearer or more suited to his or her understanding. As this process continued, both of us gained an insight to the pain and turmoil the person was going through. At the same time, they would start to give me assumptions to support the logic of the analysis, and once more they spoke and I wrote. Finally, I would be able to take them through each of the individual clouds, including the assumptions, one from each aspect of their life and gain their acceptance that I had done a good job. This always helped to create a real sense of trust between the two of us, which is critical in this relationship. More than one person acknowledged that this was the first time, in a long time, they felt someone had actually listened to them without judging them or offering platitudes. I make no judgments in this process, offer no solutions, offer none of my own experience no matter how relevant I might think it is. It is through this disciplined approach to the method, and as the story unfolds with the assumptions now clear, that they can start to take responsibility for where they are and the choices that lie before them.

The next step was to develop the composite cloud. This again took time, and I would ask them to sit beside me as I used the process already described to construct the composite cloud. At this point they were really beginning to believe that someone had listened to them, felt able to sit with them, offering an ear and a process that tried to explain why they were where they were and why they felt as they did. They were also beginning to see a causal relationship between the three, apparently separate, aspects of their life which they had never seen before. They began to see that the problems and issues of the three were indeed connected, coming together and thus adding to the pain and confusion of daily life. At the same time they were also beginning to recognize that there was a pattern appearing in each of the clouds in which a way out of the maze their life had become perhaps lay.

So we would sit and work together, trying different ways of saying the same thing and using the rigor of the process to prevent us from going off at a tangent, until the work was complete. We now had a composite cloud and we could turn our attention to the assumptions which this new level of understanding would provide. Once more I checked that what was being written met with the approval of the person. This was not always easy for the person to accept. Many times they discovered what they prob-ably knew all along, that their situation was of their own making. It was they who would have to change before any progress could be made. This really is looking into the mirror of life and having to accept at least some responsibility for the current situation.

Having gained the acceptance of the analysis so far I would then con-vert the composite cloud into a CCRT and once more invite the person to check it with me. At this point I really wanted to be sure of the robustness of the analysis. I ensured that all the CLRs were understood and used, for this is no place to cut corners and be slipshod in application; far too much is at stake. So any changes, words added or removed, were carried out until we were both satisfied. I have to be satisfied that the logic is sound; the individual has to feel that this truly is her, or his, story. This analysis, once read and understood, really is the answer to the two questions from Stations 1 and 2 of the cycle. Now the person knew what was causing many of the problems in their life, and they could also see why. It was at this point that they could also see so clearly, perhaps for the first time in a long time, that there was a way forward. There was a way out of the place they were in. They were not condemned to stay where they were, but rather, if they chose to, they could be set free from this place. It might not be easy, it might involve making hard choices, but the opportunity was there and they could see it.

Thus, when the core problem holding them back and affecting all three aspects of their life was clear, they could start to paint a compelling picture going forward. They knew some of the DEs now stood so tantalizingly close and achievable. I invited them to make a choice, "what do you want to do now?" As we already know, the choice made now determines the decisions that follow, that they will have to face in the future. More often than not they would be only too aware of the decisions they would have to make if they were to break free. But now, when goals long given up were once more within their grasp, I could see them allow the desire to achieve their goal in life be given a new life, rekindled, reborn. This was a new opportunity for them to do what they had always wanted to do, what they had set out to do, to achieve, all those years ago. This is a truly compelling picture, but they still had to choose. If they chose to stay where they were, they knew the consequences of that choice. If they decided to change, again they began to understand the consequences of that choice. Often I would leave them, sometimes for a period of time, to make the choice. I simply waited.

When they returned and sought my help in moving forward, we then started to flesh out the compelling picture in more detail. Seeking out the decisions that would still have to be made, the changes that must take place for the DEs to be achieved. Rarely is there only one change! Usually there are a number; they have to be identified, articulated clearly, thought through, and having completed that step it is possible to construct the core Future Reality Tree (FRT), linking the changes to the DEs. Once this was constructed, it was checked using the CLRs and again I invited the person to read it with me, checking it, and changing words where suggested while keeping the logic intact. Once this was finished, the compelling picture was then robust, grounded in the mind of the person and ready, once they were ready, to be transformed into a plan. This included the steps that must be followed for the changes to be completed, the actions contained at each step in logic and time dependency. For this, I use two more tools of the TOC/TP toolset, the Prerequisite Tree (PRT) and the Transition Tree (TRT). This also includes an understanding of the resources needed and the timescales involved. All that remained to be done would be to make it happen.

This was not the end of my involvement however. I was able to continue coaching as the changes took place. Sometimes additional changes were required and they needed to be inserted into the plan, and then verified. Sometimes there were other problems as not all decisions are easy, so one or two fall into the category that forms a "conflict of subordination." These had to be dealt with in the proper manner. I helped to check the key measures—the arrival of the DEs and the departure of the UDEs. By this I mean that when the person makes the necessary changes, it is likely that before the expected Desirable Effects (DEs) have been achieved, the impact, indeed the presence, of the Undesirable Effects (UDEs) starts to diminish—there is a time lag as part of the changes taking place. There is only one further step in the process—time to reflect.

This was often very moving. I have usually asked the person to keep a journal of the journey, and in the journal to capture the experiences, the emotions, and the images that came to mind as the journey unfolded. The journey so described becomes the story from where the person was at the start to where they are now, and where they can expect to be in the short and middle term. I never asked them to show me the journal, never asked to see it, nor invited them to tell me about it. It was personal to them. If they offered to show it to me I would say yes, but only if they were sure. It was their story, their journey, their hopes and aspirations. It was their relationships that were being restored. It was they who were achieving a new balance in their life. So by following the five-step reflection process they had captured the pathway from brokenness to fullness. They knew they had to keep on with the process. There would still be much to do, still many changes to be made, but they had broken free from the place where they felt trapped. Goals and aspirations once out of reach were now back in view, and with diligence would be possible to attain. This was, and is, a life transformed. They had changed, and in the changing, I often saw a new person, a new leader, ready to take on new challenges, and lead by example, with conviction.

A FINAL THOUGHT

Smith and Shaw (2011) argue that "the way we maintain the highest values is by the leader embodying and practicing them relentlessly and consistently" (p. 7), a sentiment fully endorsed by Covey (2004). Remember it is axiomatic, indeed imperative, that the leader sets, by his or her example, the standards and values of the organization. Sometimes I have found it useful to ask people to define what they themselves find both inspirational and motivational. Many times the answers come from outside the world of work, maybe the arts, sport, politics, or religion. I then ask them to compare what they have written with the goal and objectives of their organization, their team even, and ask whether they find these to be inspirational and motivational, and if not why is that? This is particularly true when it is the leader doing the analysis! If the values the leader proclaims are not evident, not inspirational, not motivational to those around him or her, then what is gained? What legacy can possibly follow?

REFERENCES AND FURTHER READING

Belbin, R. M. *Management Teams: Why They Succeed or Fail,* 2nd ed. Oxford, UK: Elsevier Butterworth Heinemann, 2004.
Covey, S. R. *The 7 Habits of Highly Effective People*. London: Simon & Schuster, 2004.
Myers-Briggs, I. *Introduction to Type,* 6th ed. Oxford, UK: CPP, 2000.
Smith, A., and P. Shaw. *The Reflective Leader*. Norwich, UK: Canterbury Press, 2011.

7

Making It Happen—Or Not

SO WHAT HAPPENED NEXT?

It is appropriate that we return to the case studies, consider what happened in each case, and then reflect upon what happened. Before we do, however, we will see a report I was recently sent from a small manufacturing company I had spent some time with in 2010. Knowing I was writing this book, I had simply asked the leader of the operations function to let me know what was taking place, a kind of update since my last time with them. This is what he wrote: *"Things are good but massively busy."* He then presented the following highlights:

Virtually all of the manufacturing processes are run using replenishment.

1. We have three replenishment "warehouses" that pull the process. Raw material, components, and finished goods (FG). We also have a midprocess replenishment warehouse for lock center cases. Not sure if this is the classical use of replenishment but it works well.

2. We are making 25 k locks per week. At this level, the constraint is still the market.

3. We are planning to drive this up to 30 k per week, and at that level we will have an internal constraint = flexi presses. We are therefore doing Single Minute Exchange of Dies (SMED) and Total Preventive Maintenance (TPM) projects on the four flexi-presses. However, even if we make significant improvements to available production time I still anticipate the need for investment in a fifth flexi. The SMED and TPM work will then pay for part of the capex justification.

4. We only use two key metrics to measure the success of our manufacturing processes
   a. On-Time in Full (OTIF) = Customer service. Owned by final assembly supervisor
   b. Stock turnover = process efficiency. Owned by lead scheduler
5. Our external OTIF is at 96 percent with a target for the end of the year of 98 percent.
6. Our stock turns are around four and our year-end target is six (a 50 percent improvement).
7. Our continuous improvement drivers are:
   a. OTIF—We measure OTIF over the five main business sectors (lock, keep, letter plate, patio lock, plastic components). If the OTIF is less than the target for the month for any area the final assembly supervisor does a root cause analysis of the missed lines. Corrective action is then implemented. So far we have generally been ahead of the target so no actions have yet been required.
   b. Stock—We now have an analysis by the same work groups as for OTIF. This analysis also has a second dimension which is to look at the location of the stock (WIP) in each of the processes. The lead scheduler and I interrogate this data and look where the high value levels of stock are. We then work with the TOC team to establish why the stock is there and ask whether we can redesign the process to reduce stock but still maintain OTIF. The first action point from this has been to drive stock off the shop floor and back into the replenishment warehouse (WIP stores); we are now in the process of redesigning the replenishment system.
8. Forty employees have completed National Vocational Qualification (NVQ) level 2 in business improvement which included eight real-life projects. Everyone passed and it was a great success.

So having spent time following the coaching cycle, answering the questions it poses, training people in the relevant tools and techniques, not just TOC tools but also those from Lean and DMAIC (Define, Measure, Analyze, Improve, Control), creating a core team, a flight crew, and giving them the responsibility to make decisions and execute them, the operations director, the leader of this team, was able to make substantial improvement. There is still much to do, but they know how to do it for themselves. They know what they are capable of and the steps they need to take. They know this project has opened up new possibilities not available to them before. It may not have been by the book but it worked for them, and still does. But it is not always like this, and now we shall return to the case studies and see what the results were.

We introduced one case study from a manufacturing company, which we left at the end of Chapter 3 and then, in Chapter 4, two from the MRO environment and one from healthcare. They had all worked their way through a full analysis of the problems and issues affecting them on their journey to the goal. They had been able to determine the core problem. They had communicated that analysis to more members of their own team and to a wider group within the organization as a whole. They had been able to paint a compelling picture to this wider group the aim of which was to gain the buy-in of those affected by the continuing problems and also of those who had to approve the strategy going forward. They had to make some choices, some decisions, and implement changes, but what did happen?

The two case studies from MRO are perhaps the best place to start. The first case study looked at the availability of key SKUs to the points of consumption. The conflict was between the current fragmented and disconnected approach that applied to all SKUs required in the MRO facility. The CCRT had highlighted that conflict and the two main drivers were quickly identified. The first was the need to develop a Lean supply chain, one that enabled a reduction in overall costs, taking out the waste that most people in the whole chain recognized was present. This was in line with corporate policy so had the support of key senior managers throughout the organization. Much time and investment had already been made in the area of Lean and DMAIC with people being trained in the various tools and techniques contained within both methodologies and intervention projects set up to aid with the appropriate transfer of knowledge. So it might be thought that this was all very promising and that the need to create a holistic, systemic approach to the provision of all SKUs would be relatively simple to develop and implement.

However, I did say there were two drivers, so we need to examine the second, namely the measurement systems in place throughout the organization and beyond into the supply chain. The existing system was dominated by the requirement for all managers to meet local optima measurement, predominately local efficiency. These measurements broke the organization down into a number of discrete entities each with a requirement to maximize its performance with respect to its capability. This took no notice of the interdependencies between these discrete entities; it simply required, indeed demanded, that they all work at what one manager described as 100 percent all the time! This was interpreted in the purchasing department as always getting the cheapest deal which meant buying in bulk, often very large bulk! This meant reducing transportation costs to a minimum, so waiting until the truck was full before shipping and so on. There were then implications for the storage of such vast amounts, often incurring an expense that came out of a different budget and therefore did not figure, or was recognized, in the purchasing price of the items. Over the years, I have met companies who have chased a large reduction in the price per part supplied without taking into account the consequence of such a driver resulting in warehouses packed full of "stuff" that remains there for a very long time indeed—but at least it was cheap! I do not want to expand too much on this here, but suffice it to say that this approach is not uncommon, indeed is all too common. So from the standpoint of this first case study, although the core issue affecting the performance of the MRO facility with respect to the provision of all SKUs used within the facility was clear, the dominance of the measurement system and the way contractual relationships were constructed in line with those measurements prevented the solution from being implemented. The issues still exist at the time of writing, and probably will for some time. The behaviors are still in line with the measures, and many relationships have broken down.

So what about the second case study from MRO? This case study had come to the conclusion that the core conflict was between the current low level of operational effectiveness and the high level of operational effectiveness required by the client. This high level of service expectation had, as a primary measure, a requirement for fast Turnaround Time (TAT). It should be remembered that the current TAT at the time of writing the case study was much longer than the tolerance time of the client. In these environments, there is always pressure to return equipment back into service. In this case study one of the key problems lay in the inability of the supply chain to provide parts needed for the repair to arrive before the time required in the maintenance bay schedule. This led to those items required being removed from equipment further back in the flow with the hope that by the time the equipment which had been robbed needed to have the parts put back the parts would have arrived through the supply chain—in most cases, this proved to be a forlorn hope.

However, on the positive side, there was a clear desire to consider just what could be achieved through the use of the tools and techniques of Lean, DMAIC, and TOC to enable such fast TAT. They had seen what was happening in other industries, some similar to theirs and others not, and could see how this would work for them. They constructed a sound and compelling picture based on the analysis they had done and were keen to make the necessary changes. But there was a further problem to that of parts supply noted previously. The facility was given the work schedule from outside, with no notice being taken of internal capability. The contractual relationship between the facility and the clients, both in terms of the loading and also the spare parts provision, lay outside of the facility; therefore they had no real control over what came in, what could be worked on, and when it might be returned to service. The supply chain management function was responsible for the provision of the components required as spare parts, and also for the way in which unserviceable parts arrived for repair. As with the previous case study there was little or no systemic understanding of how the whole MRO facility operated within the context of both the client and the supply base. Once more the dominant way of working was rooted in the maximization of local optima, everyone working at 100 percent and penalized when they did not comply. So what happened was that the constantly changing priorities continued to change, the level of WIP rose, and the TAT went up. So although the result of the analysis was to develop a compelling picture of how it might be, from which the necessary changes were developed and known, thus the opportunity was there, different choices were made and the performance gap was not closed. As with the previous case study relationships had broken down, and the level of dysfunctional behavior was high.

But what about the case study from the healthcare environment? Surely that had a different outcome. Well, no! The core conflict was not that dissimilar to that of the second MRO case study, it being that the current mode of operation was fragmented in terms of alignment, consistency of purpose, and systemic understanding, and was in conflict with the need for the mode of operation to be aligned in terms of consistency of purpose and systemic understanding. Once more the compelling picture had been developed and communicated, and an outline implementation plan developed. However, it rapidly became obvious that no progress would be made in the implementation of such a plan. It did not matter how robust our analysis had been, or how appealing the compelling picture was, there were other considerations to be taken into account that had not been included. Within the context of the hospital there were powerful forces for maintaining the status quo, vested interests that would not permit such changes, and too many conflicting interests all with their own measurement as to how the organization should be managed, led, and measured. With each department chasing their own local optima there was no encouragement to see the organization as a whole entity. The belief that such an organization should be seen in terms of interdependency, which is so critical, was, at the same time, not accepted nor even considered. W. Edwards Deming, back in 1993, wrote about this in his book entitled *The New Economics* (1994), and it is well worth reading today as the message is no less powerful with the passage of time; indeed, it is perhaps fair to say that it is more relevant today than ever before. It is also a message that Goldratt made clear in much of his writing and conference presentations (e.g., Goldratt and Fox, 1986). The dysfunctional behaviors that both Deming and Goldratt forecast can be readily seen in almost all types of organization, including hospitals.

Such is the dominance of the "local optima" measurement paradigm coupled with the assumption that the sum of the local optima equals the global optima seems to be so rooted in organizations today that the erroneous nature of the assumption and the devastating, consequential impact of the rigorous application of such a measurement system is missed. Yet all organizations are systems and as such demand a systemic approach to both leadership and measurement.

The dominant, local optima view contends that only by breaking down such a large and complex organization could control ever be exercised, could the goal of the organization ever be achieved. Therefore, make each person responsible for maximizing their own bit and the sum of all these bits would make for a successful hospital; this was the assumption upon which the whole was to be managed and led. Flow of patients through the system was secondary to the achievement of the local measures, and then there was more complication. The hospital operated in the context of the Department of Health, local administration through Primary Care Trusts, and substantial political intrusion at both local and national levels. This combination certainly added to the complexity of managing the hospital, and the sheer numbers of measures, with many of them conflicting, only added further to the general sense of confusion. It should also be noted that these outside influences also subscribe to the dominant view of local optima. The result from the case study was that the solution developed by the internal team was not implemented, and the expected results, were that solution to have been implemented, were not achieved. In the case of this organization, the dominant view of how to run such an organization won over the new approach being proposed and the problems remained.

I will return to the first case study in Chapter 8, but now want to turn to an examination as to why, in the examples shown in the case studies, the results were as they were and not as had been hoped. They had all completed a sound analysis of the problems and issues, and they had all arrived at the point where they were able to develop the compelling picture and the implementation plan to turn the picture into reality, but nothing happened, nothing changed other than for the worse.

SO WHY DOES THIS HAPPEN? A QUESTION OF PARADIGMS

In my research at Cranfield University some fifteen years ago, the question of paradigms became recognized as critical to making good choices. Examining what I felt to be the primary barrier to change in that research led to the definition of the concept I defined as paradigm lock. I found this to be a really powerful block on managing effective change of all kinds. As part of the original research data capture, paradigm lock was found in DBR implementations, in critical chain implementations, and in enterprise solution implementations. The data set for this research comprised over four hundred people, in over thirteen companies throughout Europe and the United States. My colleagues at the time then validated my findings by confirming the same major barrier to change. My book *Unconstrained Organisations* (2001) provides a full description of the research, the methods employed for data capture and analysis, and the conclusions drawn. Over the years since that research was completed I have continued to capture data that confirms the existence of paradigm lock and its continuing impact. It seemed appropriate then to return in this book to the whole question of paradigms and how people can become so locked into one that they, their team, and often their organization can become so sub-optimal that the whole operation ceases to be effective.

PARADIGM LOCK OVERVIEW

The impact of paradigm lock is discussed more fully in *Unconstrained Organisations;* however, a brief description is of value. In the research, the basic question asked was why, when a full and implementable solution has been properly developed and everyone is ready to make it happen, does nothing happen? The whole of the data set was drawn from people who had attended programs I was running at the time, using the TOC/TP to develop such solutions for the major problems affecting their company at the time. They had followed the steps of the TP, from UDE all the way through to the detailed plans for achieving the DEs, with the full support of all the team. Yet they failed to gain anything like the results they, and I, expected.

I developed a simple change model that suggested a dysfunctional response to the solution being presented. This response was clearly a conflict between "implement the solution" against "don't implement the solution." When this conflict could not be resolved I was able to show that the primary cause for this nonresolution lay with the individual blocking the change; being "locked" into a paradigm which was stronger than the desire to implement the change itself. Using the data set, comprising over three hundred conflict clouds, I was able to reduce that number to one single cloud—the Paradigm Lock cloud. I then spoke to those who had taken part in the research to validate my analysis, which they were able to do.

The cloud is shown in Figure 7.1. The basic reading of the cloud states, "**In order to** *achieve my goal in life* **I must** *deal with the constraints that block me*, and **in order to** *deal with the constraints that block me*, **I must** *change my paradigm with respect to...*" Here is where the sticking issue is placed. Then I read the top part of the cloud. "**In order to** *achieve my goal in life* **I**

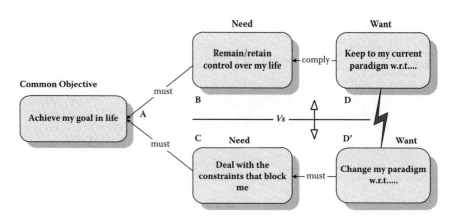

FIGURE 7.1
Paradigm lock cloud.

must *remain in/retain control over my life*, and **in order to** *remain in/retain control over my life* **I must not** *change my paradigm with respect to…*"

The conflict is clear. I cannot both keep to a paradigm and change that paradigm at the same point in time. I have to choose one or the other. If I stay with the current paradigm then clearly the logic says that I will still be in control over my life; however if I do make this choice then I clearly cannot deal with the constraints that block my progress toward my goal in life, and I am forced to accept that I am going to stay where I am and not move forward. This in turn leads me to the inevitable conclusion that whatever my goal in life might have been, it is no longer open to me. We might consider that there are other options which could be chosen and do lead to the goal; however the individual trapped in paradigm lock does not see those other options. So the next step is to consider the assumptions that hold this conflict in place. These too must be surfaced and understood.

The assumptions raised show the devastating impact of the cloud and the real impact of the cross-connection (see Figure 7.2). The full power of the cloud can now be seen. So, I might argue that today I have a core problem, I have done all the analysis, and the core problem is clear and

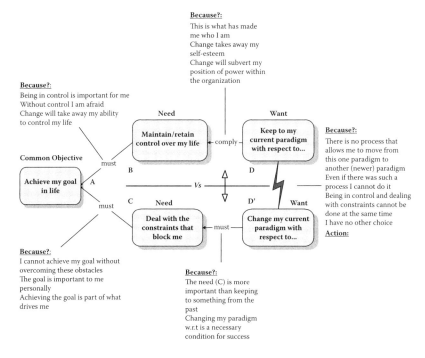

FIGURE 7.2
Paradigm lock cloud with assumptions.

unequivocal. In other words I have completed both Stations 1 and 2 of the coaching cycle. I want to have the solution, in other words move from D to D', and I have completed Stations 3 and 4 of the coaching cycle, I have the compelling picture fully developed, and all reservations have been noted and properly dealt with. I am ready to lead my team, my team is ready to go, and my organization is ready to see the closing of the performance gap. Only now there is a problem, and the solution about to be implemented challenges one of my most precious paradigms. In other words, D' is now recognized as being a fundamental challenge to what is written in the B box, and there is only one conclusion for me to draw from this: I cannot move to D', I cannot violate this paradigm, I cannot lead this change, I cannot allow it to happen, and it must be stopped. But, the new paradigm is a necessary condition for my leading the whole organization forward, leading my team forward, and that is therefore a necessary condition for the achievement of the goal, my goal, the team goal, and the organizational goal. I know that if I stay with the old paradigm, then C is out of the question, and therefore A is also no longer possible. This is the lock created by the cloud.

Although B and C are not in conflict, they never are in any cloud, and although A is what I really want, I am blocked from moving to D', but why? At the time of the original research, I considered there to be two forces preventing me from moving. The first is that I cannot see how both B and C can exist at the same time; I can have one or the other but not both. The second is that even if it were possible to have both at the same time, there is no process available to enable that to take place, and there is no obvious solution to this problem, no system that allows me to move to the new paradigm while not violating the continued existence of the statement in the B box. The analysis that I have done does lay before me a choice however. I can change my paradigm to a new paradigm, one which allows me to address the constraint(s) holding me back from my goal. But in so doing, the perception is that such a change of paradigm harms my understanding of who I am, of what I stand for, of that which allows me to feel in control over my life—such a change of paradigm is therefore not to be countenanced under any circumstance. Therefore, I am faced with a terrible choice: stay as I am and give up on my goal in life, or change my paradigm, which robs me of my perception of who I am and how others see me.

As there is no solution to this impasse, all that is left for me to focus on is the B box. I must remain in control no matter what. I will control everything if I can and thus prevent the change to a new, different, and highly damaging to me, paradigm. The original research showed that many had given up on the statement in the A box and only focused on maintaining what was written in the B box. They were locked into the current paradigm and nothing could change them. However what was perhaps the saddest aspect of this position was that they had given up on their goals. Both during the time of the original research, and since, I have met so many people who have given up on their goal in life.

At the time, I set out to develop a solution to this problem and came up with three injections, three major changes that might, and in many cases did, overcome the impact of paradigm lock for some people. These three key injections for addressing paradigm lock were as follows:

1. **Subordinate to the goal/constraint**: This might seem obvious, but in the work I was doing as part of personal focus (see Chapter 6), being able to invite them to talk to me about their goals in life, not just work but across the whole spectrum—work, family, and community—allowed them to wax lyrical about what they had hoped for. Remember they had considered that such goals were unachievable and had long since given up on them. But they remained deep inside the person, an untold story that kept pulling them back, often wistfully, and here was I, opening that opportunity once more. In that discussion and through the use of the personal focus approach, I have often found it possible to open up the opportunity once more for a new journey toward their goal. It may not be exactly as it once was, as time moves on, but to see eyes being raised to a new, and often higher, plane is wonderful to watch.

2. **Take responsibility, and be accountable, for the results of my actions**: I had once thought that the key here was the action itself, but no, it is the results of the actions that must be recognized, must be accepted, and responsibility taken for. It is too easy here to blame someone, anyone, as long as the finger does not point at me. In the discussions it was relatively straightforward to lead people gently to the place where they had to admit to themselves that the real cause of their inability to achieve what they had set out to achieve was actually themselves. This is never an easy state to accept, and needs very careful handling, but the journey is worth the time and energy spent on it. "What do I have to do?" is the question they would often ask at this point.

3. **Give, and respond to, leadership**: I kept coming back to this, as at the time it seemed the easy option. I knew that leadership is not a function of hierarchy. But just how ready are people to first of all give leadership, and then, how able are they to accept, or respond to, leadership? I had worked closely with people in the personal focus approach and in that work found that many were not used to responding to leadership—giving it yes, but responding no!

Although I found that these three changes were often successful in helping the person to break free from the grip of paradigm lock, I also knew of many for whom such a change was beyond them. They were still eager to try and change but found the journey far too difficult. In trying to understand the complexities of this I set out to understand more about how our various paradigms come to exist in the first place and why some are so difficult to change.

THE IMPORTANCE OF WORLDVIEW

The whole concept of "worldview" lies at the heart of how we interpret the world around us. Thus we have the concept of a worldview that then informs our mindset for the areas in which we are working and from that mindset our basic beliefs are formed. These basic beliefs, or basic assumptions as I call them, are the bedrock of our value system and the lens through which we see the world. They determine all our relationships, at home, at work, and the wider community. This pathway then, from worldview to basic assumptions, provides the platform that informs the choices we make (see Figure 7.3).

Few choices are made that do not in some way conform to the basic assumptions by which, and through which, we see the world around us. The pathway by which our worldview is formed is not the subject of this book, but clearly our background, our education, the community in which we grew up, all combine to create within us our worldview. As we grow older this can change, develop, become clearer, become more entrenched perhaps. Whatever the process, as we move into the world of work, these influences on our life become the foundation for what follows. Of course, many influences are highly positive and help us to become part of the human family on Earth; however, not all are so. There are those that are

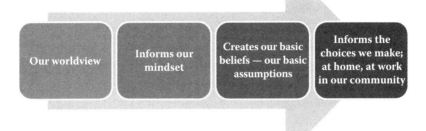

FIGURE 7.3
Worldview to basic assumptions and making choices.

clearly negative, at least from a societal perspective. Again this is not the primary focus of this book, as we are looking at leadership, but the fact remains that we should always remember that the process by which our basic assumptions are formed has implications way beyond the world of work. But what is a worldview?

A worldview is often defined as the fundamental cognitive orientation of an individual or society encompassing natural philosophy, or themes, values, emotions, and ethics. It is a concept which is fundamental to and refers to a wide world perception, what is often described as conventional wisdom. It can also refer to a framework of ideas and beliefs through which an individual interprets the world and interacts with it.

When applied to a group of people such as a team the term "worldview" can be expressed as the fundamental cognitive, affective, and evaluative presuppositions the team make about the nature of things, and which they use to order their lives, make the choices, and make the decisions that follow, and finally the life within the team and/or the organization in which they work. It is from our worldview that beliefs are formed, and thus the relationship to actions. It is felt that we tend to internalize the beliefs of the people around us during childhood. Albert Einstein is often quoted as having said, "Common sense is the collection of prejudices acquired by age eighteen."

There are times when the people within a team or organization may adopt the beliefs of a charismatic leader, or one with great power over those below him or her, even if those beliefs fly in the face of all previous beliefs, and produce actions that are clearly not in their own self-interest. This is when we can see a conflict of beliefs, when the paradigm of one is clearly in conflict with the paradigm of another. I have found that people who are more than capable of developing their own set of beliefs and are well aware of the process by which beliefs form, still cling strongly to those beliefs, and act on them, even when this is against their own self-interest.

Many years ago when I studied both decision theory and general systems theory, I became very much aware of the development of a mindset, a set of assumptions or methods held by an individual, or a team, or even a wider group which can be so established that it creates a powerful incentive within these people or groups to continue to adopt or accept prior behaviors, choices, or tools. This is particularly prevalent within the army, which is where I first came across the whole area of leadership and what it meant at the time.

PARADIGMS: THE DISCUSSION GOES DEEPER

The whole area of paradigms first captured my attention when I researched the area of change and the application of the TOC to the process of managing change. During the time of my research at Cranfield, I came across Thomas Kuhn, who really developed the use of the word "paradigm" in its current setting. He used the word to refer to the set of practices that define a scientific discipline at any particular period of time. In his book, Kuhn (1970) defines a scientific paradigm as

1. *What* is to be observed and scrutinized, which leads to
2. The kind of *questions* that are supposed to be asked and probed for answers in relation to this subject, which in turn leads to
3. *How* these questions are to be structured, and then finally
4. *How* the results of scientific investigations should be interpreted.

One important aspect of Kuhn's definition of a paradigm is that when examining the same environment, two such paradigms are incommensurable, meaning two paradigms cannot be reconciled with each other because they cannot be subjected to the same common standard of comparison. They are in conflict. This can apply at more than one level:

1. The conflict between my personal paradigm and that of the team
2. The conflict between my personal paradigm and that of the organization
3. The conflict between my team paradigm and that of the organization

In each of these three cases, it is possible to both predict and then witness the sequence of events that such unresolved conflicts create. No meaningful comparison between the competing paradigms is possible without a fundamental modification of the concepts that are an intrinsic part of each the paradigms being compared. This way of looking at the concept of "paradigm" creates a paradox of sorts, since competing paradigms are in fact constantly being measured against each other. This definition, however, makes it clear that the real barrier to comparison is not necessarily the absence of common units of measurement, but an absence of mutually compatible or mutually intelligible concepts.

A simplified analogy for *paradigm* is a habit of reasoning, or "the box" in the commonly used phrase "thinking outside the box." Thinking inside the box is analogous with normal practice, the way things are usually done, the application of conventional wisdom. The box encompasses the thinking of normal approaches and thus the box is analogous with the *dominant paradigm*. "Thinking outside the box" would be what Kuhn calls revolutionary science. Revolutionary science is usually unsuccessful, and very rarely leads to new paradigms. However, when existing paradigms are succesfully challenged they lead to large-scale changes in the scientific worldview. When these large-scale shifts in the scientific view are implemented and accepted by the majority, it will then become "the box" and science will progress within it. The same applies to organizational, team, and individual development. Much of what this book is about focuses on the need often to challenge, and then change, a dominant paradigm.

Another use of the word *paradigm* is in the social sciences where the term is used to describe the set of experiences, beliefs, and values that affect the way an individual perceives reality and responds to that perception. The phrase "paradigm shift" has been used to denote a change in how a given society goes about organizing and understanding reality. A "dominant paradigm" refers to the values, structures, or systems of thought in a society that are common and widely held at any given point in time. Thus dominant paradigms are shaped both by the community's cultural background and by the context of the historical moment. This is of great value when exploring how people make choices within organizations, in particular those that have a strong identity and have adopted powerful, dominant paradigms in order to maintain order and stability.

I have found the following aspects to be of particular importance. Professional membership organizations often give legitimacy to the dominant paradigm through their training and rules for becoming a member. Then there are those dynamic leaders who introduce and promote the paradigm, pushing it at every opportunity, making sure that everyone within the organization follows the dominant paradigm even if it might be in conflict with their personal paradigms. This also applies to the many professional journalists and editors who write about the system of thought and how it is, or should be, applied within any given context. They both disseminate the information essential to the paradigm and give the paradigm legitimacy and cull any material that conflicts with their own paradigm, thus ensuring that alternative approaches have great difficulty in gaining any credence. Often I have found that government departments give credence to a paradigm even when the evidence from other sources has begun to promote a different paradigm. The level of entrenched opinion here is high as is the level of inertia. The dominant paradigm is also supported by lecturers and teachers who propagate the paradigm's ideas by teaching it to students, setting the reading lists to confirm the dominant paradigm and excluding any alternatives. This is often compounded by conferences that present ideas central to the paradigm. Finally, there is media coverage where the dominant paradigm is given prominence, and any alternatives, if they are lucky enough to feature, are given only a short amount of time or are ridiculed by those from the dominant paradigm. Once this powerful process is in place then it is no wonder that those who do not have either the time or the access to alternatives promote the dominant paradigm without any thought that there might be a better way. For a great description of how a dominant paradigm can affect changing an organization, try Ray Immelman's 2003 book *Great Boss, Dead Boss*, in which he covers just how the tribal behaviors of people within organization are enshrined and consequently put the brake on any change program.

Covey (2004) also notes the impact of paradigms. He argues strongly that a paradigm can be seen as a map, one which offers explanations of certain aspects of the territory we are looking at. Covey recognizes the importance of making a paradigm shift, thus echoing Kuhn. He also confirms my own view that many people today feel lost. This has, as noted by Covey (2004), "nothing to do with your behavior or your attitude. It has everything to do with you having the wrong map" (p. 24). This notion resonates well with my own findings which confirm that many people refuse to change the map, clinging to it as if their life depended on it. Yet it remains the wrong map. This is an excellent definition of the situation, or condition, people suffer from when locked into the wrong paradigm. Covey then goes on to state, "We interpret everything we experience through these mental maps: maps of the way things are, as realities, and maps of the way things should be, our values. We seldom question their accuracy; we're usually even unaware that we have them, we simply assume that the way we see things is the way they really are, or the way they should be" (p. 24).

The impact of our basic assumptions, our basic paradigms, is substantial. Covey notes, "The more aware we are of our basic paradigms….and the extent to which we have been influenced by our experience, the more we can take responsibility for those paradigms, listen to others, and be open to their perception, thereby getting a larger picture and a far more objective view" (p. 29). Covey continues, "Paradigms are powerful because they create the lens through which we see the world. The power of the paradigm shift is the essential power of a quantum change, whether that shift is instantaneous or a slow and deliberate process" (p. 32). It is always interesting to discover that as you study a particular aspect in one field of inquiry, another field, which you may think to be very different, is encountered where the similarities are both powerful and insightful. In this case, in my theological studies I came across similar issues related to worldviews and paradigms in that field which illuminated my understanding in the world of organizations and leadership.

THE FOUR ELEMENTS OF A WORLDVIEW

One of the leading theologians in this understanding of worldview and the impact it has on the way people think, and act, is Tom Wright of the University of St. Andrews and a former Bishop of Durham. For Wright (2004) a worldview "embraces all deep-level perceptions of reality" (p. 123), and he then goes on to argue that "there are four things which worldviews characteristically do, in each of which the entire worldview can be glimpsed" these being Stories, Basic Questions, Symbols, and finally Praxis, shown in Figure 7.4.

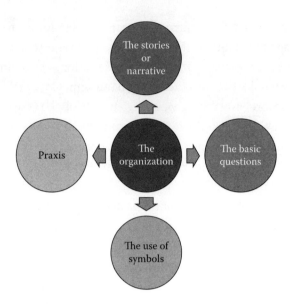

FIGURE 7.4
The interaction within a worldview.

Stories: This is all about narrative. All the organizations I have studied over the years have such stories that capture just what it (the organization) is about; these are sometimes the myths and legends that organizations create or simply a statement of how things are done. The stories reflect a deeply held expression of the dominant worldview within the organization, and act as a litmus test for the way forward. This is where the identity of the organization is drawn from. I discussed the importance of stories in the Introduction, and what Wright is talking about, albeit from a different environment, resonates with what was said then. Stories become the tradition of the organization, and they are part of the history as to how we got where we are. This is particularly true of regiments in the army, in which the history of the regiment is drummed into every new recruit until they, too, become part of the story. The story is also dynamic in that it is expected that new examples of the story, reinforcing the tradition, will be incorporated into the original, thus ensuring that the tradition so described will remain robust and not be lost.

Basic Questions: It is in the stories that the answers to basic questions are drawn; the phrase "that's not how we do things around here" is a good example, or the opposite, "this is how we do things around here," laying out to any newcomer just how the organization functions, makes decisions. This is where we are able to say to any-one that this is who we are, why we exist, what we do, and so on. This is as much cultural as anything else. Wright argues that there are four questions that must be answered, "who are we; where are we; what is wrong and what is the solution" (p. 123). It is from the world-view that the answers to these questions are derived.

Symbols: This is a fascinating area to examine. Many organizations develop their own symbols that reflect the journey that they have taken from the start. These symbols also act as boundary markers, giving confidence and identity to those inside, and a barrier to those outside. Wright suggests that "these symbols, as acted and visible reminders of a worldview that normally remains too deep for casual speech, form the actual grids through which the world is perceived. They determine how, from day to day, human beings will view the whole of reality" (p. 124). The story, coupled with the answers to the basic questions is translated into symbols. Today the paradigm of banking is seen in the buildings, the rewards, the bonuses, the life-style of those who are rooted in that worldview. In the developed world, we see the symbols of that worldview in the trappings of suc-cess, the power that is bestowed and the influence obtained in the corridors of power.

Praxis: This is the process by which a theoretical approach or lesson is translated into action. It is where a skill is enacted, practiced, embodied, or realized. While praxis usually refers to the process of putting this theoretical knowledge into practice, the strategic and organizational usage of the word emphasises the need for a constant cycle of conceptualizing the meanings of what can be learned from experience in order to reframe strategic and operational models. This is, as Wright describes it, "a way-of-being-in-the-world" (p. 124). Wright argues that "the real shape of someone's worldview can often be seen in the sort of actions they perform, particularly if the actions are so instinctive or habitual as to be taken for granted. The choice of a life-aim—to make money, to raise a family, to pursue a vocation, to change society or the world in a particular way, to live in harmony with the created order, to develop one's own inner world, to be loyal to received traditions—reflects the worldview held; and so do the intentions and motivations with which the overall aim goes to work" (p. 124).

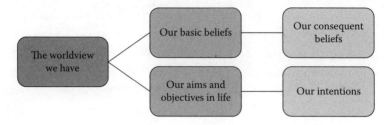

FIGURE 7.5
Worldviews, aims, and basic beliefs.

Wright goes on to make the following observation which resonates with my own research: "Inconsistency of aim and action does not invalidate this, but merely shows that the issue is complicated, and that the answer to the third question, what is wrong should certainly include human muddledness" (p. 124). For Wright worldviews are "thus the basic stuff of human existence, the lens through which the world is seen, the blueprint for how one should live in it, and above all the sense of identity and place which enables human beings to be what they are" (p. 124). Praxis is the visible manifestation of the worldview that lies at its heart. Over time the outward signs might change, the actions taken may be tempered by external opinion or a changing set of beliefs that appear to challenge the worldview, but these are superficial changes that do not affect the dominant worldview that lies below.

Wright (2004) argues that "Worldviews normally come into sight, on a more day to day basis, in sets of beliefs and aims, which emerge into the open, which are more regularly discussed and which in principle could be revised somewhat without revising the worldview itself" (p. 125). Wright recognizes this connection between worldview and how this is played out in real life (see Figure 7.5). He notes that the "basic beliefs and aims which serve to express and perhaps safeguard the worldview, give rise to consequent beliefs and intentions, about the world, oneself, one's society and one's god. These in their turn shade off in various directions, into opinions held and motivations acted upon with varying degrees of conviction. Many discussions, debates, and arguments take place at the level of consequent belief and intention, assuming a level of shared basic belief, and only going back there when faced with a complete stalemate" (p. 126). In the case studies, it was apparent that many times the underlying worldview perceived a challenge to its position and immediately set up defenses to ensure it remained dominant. The dominant worldview of local optima was able to withstand the pressures exerted by those offering a different way forward, trying to lead the organization in a different way, through forcing those promoting the new way to retract or face exclusion from the corridors of power and advancement. Challenging the dominant paradigm was regularly seen as career damaging in both the MRO and healthcare environment.

A CLASH OF CONSTRUCTS

This example (see Figure 7.6) is drawn from a common conflict seen in many different types of organizations. It is a clash of paradigms, or constructs, if you prefer to call it that. Reading the cloud follows the usual manner, that in order for the organization to be effective in achieving the goal/objectives set for it, there is clear command and control operating throughout the whole of the organization.

This is all about consistency of rules and procedures, and it is a recognition that only through such a scrupulous approach can any tangential

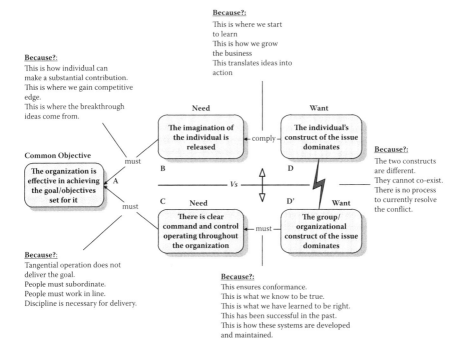

FIGURE 7.6
The conflict of constructs.

activity be stopped. It concerns the importance of subordination to the whole, the organization and how it sees itself, the importance of discipline throughout applied with complete authority. Thus, in order to ensure that such clear command and control is operating throughout the whole of the organization, the group/organizational construct must dominate. The assumptions are that this is where we can ensure such conformance, this is clearly the only way to run such a large and disparate business, this is what has led us to be successful in the past, and this is how we will maintain our progress in the future.

The analysis also recognizes the importance of the individual in that, for the organization to be effective in terms of the goal/objectives set for it, the imagination of the people must be released. The reasons for this are self-evident! This is where people can make a real contribution to the ongoing development of the business, and this is where we can develop our uniqueness, our ability to differentiate ourselves from the competition. This is where the true value lies, and in order to allow this release of imagination we must therefore allow the individual construct to dominate as this is the only way to enable to freedom of ideas we need so much at this point in our story, our journey as an organization. But there is a real and pressing problem here, for it is usually not possible to have two competing paradigms operating at the one and the same time: chaos would ensue. Even if we wanted to try and have it both ways, we do not possess a process capable of maintaining both approaches at the one and the same time.

What happens when more of the same is not going to restore the organization onto a path of on-going improvement, taking steps forward toward the goal? In other words, as the reading of the cloud reveals, in order for the organization to be effective in achieving the goal/objectives set for it the imagination of the individual must be released, and in order for that imagination to be released we must allow the individual to be free to challenge the basic assumptions, to challenge what has been done in the past and to consider the alternatives in a new light. This is for me truly transformational leadership in practice.

At the same time, it is this point of understanding, that the need to both challenge and, perhaps, break away from the dominant paradigm, becomes vital for the future well-being of the organization. I have found so many companies locked into a position from which they perceive no escape, and indeed some have closed down because they could not resolve this conflict. Many could not take this step into what they feel is the unknown; better to close than change. The strength of the dominant paradigm was so strong that first, the key people needed to see the company through left, and those that remained only kept with the old paradigm, often a discredited paradigm in other organizations, but held to here with great affection. For more on this whole aspect of paradigms and changing them, one of the best books to describe this is *Who Moved My Cheese?* by Spencer Johnson (1998).

THREE PERSPECTIVES

So we come to the final aspect I wish to consider in this chapter, understanding the three perspectives we have considered and some relevant questions to help us determine what we might do next. I consider there to be a set of basic questions that can, and should, be asked for each perspective, these being as shown here.

Seven Basic Questions

The seven basic questions are

1. Who are we?
2. Where are we?
3. Why do we exist?
4. What are we doing?
5. What is wrong?
6. What is the solution?
7. Where are we going?

These questions need to be asked in terms of the organization, the team, and myself, as shown in Figure 7.7. In each there will be a worldview. In each there will be the kind of things we have already discussed, stories, beliefs (both basic and consequent), aims, and intentions. Some will be in alignment, and some will not—but which? For example, what happens when the worldview I have is at odds with that of my team, or my organization, or both, and what if the solution I am putting forward in order to address that which is wrong at a higher level conflicts with the higher worldview, and if I am the leader of that organization, what then? It is in the answering of these questions that the coaching cycle was

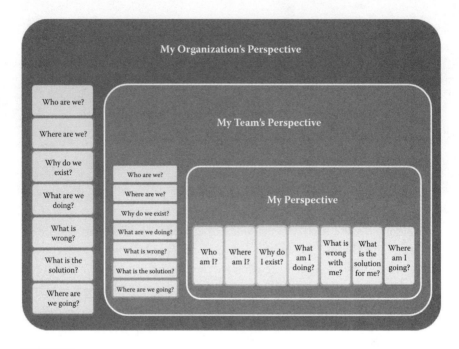

FIGURE 7.7
Questions of perspective.

developed alongside our "coaching quadrant" approach, which will be discussed in more detail in Chapter 8.

REFERENCES AND FURTHER READING

Covey, S. R. *The 7 Habits of Effective People*. London: Simon & Schuster, 2004.
Deming, W. E. *The New Economics*, 2nd ed. Cambridge, MA: MIT CAES, 1994.
Goldratt, E. M., and R. E. Fox. *The Race*. Great Barrington, MA: North River Press, 1986.
Hutchin, T. *Unconstrained Organisations*. London: Thomas Telford, 2001.
Immelman, R. *Great Boss, Dead Boss*. Gurnee, IL: Stewart Philip International, 2003.
Johnson, S. *Who Moved My Cheese?* New York: Putnam, 1998.
Kuhn, T. S. *The Structure of Scientific Revolutions*, 2nd ed. Chicago: University of Chicago Press, 1970.
Wright, N. T. *Jesus and the Victory of God*. London: SPCK, 1996.
Wright, N. T. *New Testament and the People of God*. London: SPCK, 2004.

8

Drawing It All Together

BRINGING THE MAIN CASE STUDY UP TO DATE

We left the case study of the small manufacturing company which began in Chapter 3 with their analysis of the core issues affecting performance, so now is the time to bring the story up to date. First, let's introduce the company in more detail. They are rated as one of the top five in the world for the manufacture of photo chemically machined (PCM) precision metal components. They currently manufacture 500 million components per annum and process some 25+ tons of metal per week. They employ around 190 people over two sites and have a turnover of £ 12 M. The company was established in the 1960s and uses a range of processes such as photo-etching/photo chemical machining, laser evolved etching process and laser evolved electro-forming (LEEP & LEEF), wire electrical discharge machining (EDM), three-dimensional precision components (3DPC) (bending/forming), and finally finishing and plating. The key industry sectors include electronics, aerospace and military, medical, communications, automotive, precision engineering, and energy. The company has a strategy of finding a competitive advantage through speed of supply by fast and robust delivery schedules and using strategic internal material stocks. They have a comprehensive manufacturing capability, being able to supply custom solutions coupled with a unique technology offering to clients. They have considerable volume versatility, the range being from one to one million.

They see "time to market" as a key component of their competitive edge, including design verification and evaluation with specific reference to rapid prototyping where engineers need to trial designs quickly and cost effectively. In terms of material, they hold some 2,400 material variants in stock, and stock availability can be checked at customer inquiry stage. They expect to meet the target of order receipt to job card issue in less than five minutes, coupled with the material being issued in conjunction with the tooling being produced. So there is great pressure within the company to ensure that the expectations of both client and the company itself are met. However, as you will have noted from the analysis in Chapter 3, there was a significant gap between expectation and reality. They had to change in order to grow. They had to make key decisions in terms of strategy and tactics if they were to be successful in their chosen direction of opening up both the United Kingdom and Europe without sacrificing the platform that had been created—so what did they do?

The core of the solution chosen was to implement the TOC approach for operations known as Drum Buffer Rope (DBR). This involves a series of system changes, procedural changes, and roles/responsibility changes. Central to the implementation was the development of a much more robust release process for an order, coupled with the necessary material. The project plan for the implementation included a significant amount of training throughout the company, the integration of their existing IT systems with a DBR scheduling system, the design and implementation of a new Job Card which would act as the key information source for all details relevant to each order. Much has been written elsewhere about implementing DBR which does not need to be covered here. The key aspects that I wish to focus on are the changes to the way they managed the transition, and then the on-going progress of the DBR project. They knew that the solution had to be both scalable and sustainable. They knew that engaging with the rest of the workforce would be critical and would entail training and regular communication in both directions. Their first step was to create a core team to lead the implementation.

DEVELOPING THE "FLIGHT CREW"

The idea of the "flight crew" was introduced in Chapter 5 (see Figure 8.1). The use of the flight crew approach here began with recognizing that there were two distinct crews required: one for managing the process from the receipt of each order from the client through design review, preparing the

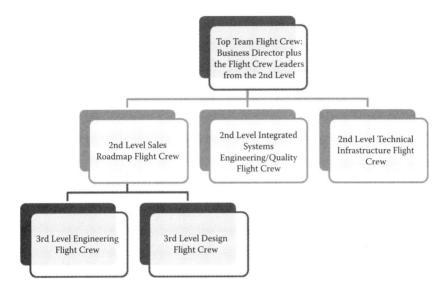

FIGURE 8.1
The flight crews.

tools through the computer aided design (CAD) department, then through "first off" to shipment. This team was called the sales roadmap flight crew. The leader of this crew also had as her key measure of performance the delivery target of 100 percent On-Time, In-Full, Right First Time (100% OTIF/RFT). Next, the second crew—the technical infrastructure flight crew—was set up. This crew was tasked with creating, developing, and maintaining of the technical infrastructure to provide the first crew with all the necessary information upon which to manage the order roadmap. This included the scheduling, the technical buffer management, load capacity analysis, and all the other technical systems required to maintain the processes used throughout the plant.

The initial team took upon themselves the task of determining who should be in each crew and the roles and responsibilities they would each have. From the implementation plan they determined who should take overall control of the key changes, who would be involved in the actions that had to be completed for the plan to be achieved, and the measures of progress to be used in such a way that everyone could see progress. Acting as a pathway of integration, they set up an Integrated Systems Engineering function that would also be responsible for maintaining all the quality systems and standards required by the client base. This function would also act as the focusing point for all interventions using either Lean or DMAIC tools as defined by the buffer management. It was in this way that they then developed the strategy for the company going forward, and then the tactics within each function in order to ensure alignment of purpose and decision making.

CHANGES TO THE ORGANIZATIONAL STRUCTURE

Once the flight crews had been formed, they were tasked with addressing the issues raised following the analysis described in Chapter 3 and then implementing the plan they had created. They moved their physical positions in the company to sitting around the same group of tables. This was the first time the company had allowed people to move into cross-functional teams. For some this meant leaving their offices and sitting out in the larger, open-plan office space. For others this meant being further away from their usual place of working, but again, the importance of the crew being together was recognized and they quickly overcame any resistance. Now, with sales, design, and engineering all sitting together issues were quickly dealt with, fewer mistakes occurred and the speed of entry to the system improved. They knew that the sum of the process times for almost all products was seventy minutes and that the current lead time was over three weeks in most cases, so they knew what they had to achieve. They were also encouraged to develop their own flight crews in order to cascade the strategy and tactics down to the shop-floor and the office staff. This helped with the alignment of decision making and lines of communication. It also allowed people to raise concerns much more effectively than before, which meant they were dealt with much more effectively than before.

MAKING IT HAPPEN

In the weeks that followed from go-live, much changed. Because of the robustness of their analysis they had a truly compelling picture to communicate, and did so. This included regular presentations to the main board of the company. As part of the work covered by Station 4 of the coaching cycle they had identified many obstacles to the proposed changes from a considerable number of people within the company. They then developed the Intermediate Objectives in order to overcome each of the obstacles, incorporating the actions that would be required. They created a project plan, properly resourced and meeting the requirements of a Critical Chain project—this was more for my benefit as I used Critical Chain to monitor progress. This allowed them to open up the crew strategy to a much wider group, engaged people in debate, and helped to create an atmosphere of win-win. They knew what they had to do. The two second-level flight crews now know what their contribution is to the whole, and can bring in such resources as are necessary to achieve the overall objectives. They are able to create their own flight crews as and when necessary and use them to continue the process of leading and managing the changes that are required. At the time of writing, good progress was being made in the implementation of the overall project plan. However, new obstacles not recognized at the beginning have surfaced as they have delved deeper into the way in which orders are processed. This has led to firstly, a review of the actions contained within the original plan with new actions being inserted into the plan in order to maintain the right direction and secondly, a far deeper understanding of how operations functions. The deeper understanding that has been achieved in this time has also added greatly to their knowledge and understanding of their supply chain and the needs of the clients, and this is now enabling them respond to new markets.

_____

REFLECTION ON THE CASE STUDY

Time will tell if they are going to be successful in terms of the solution they have developed and implemented, but it is possible to consider how they used both the coaching cycle and in particular, the final station of the cycle, review and reflect. As in all the case studies, they had started with a clear understanding of the goal and the necessary conditions to achieve it. They then recognized the performance gap and knew they had to do something.

In four months they had been able to work their way through the coaching cycle, from Stations 1 to 5. They had been able to assess some of the current UDEs affecting performance and from that to define the core issues holding them back. They tailored the solution known as DBR for their own environment, building both a robust implementation plan, and at the same time communicated what was going to happen to the workforce. Once the overall project plan was ready to go, they started and maintained progress. They had to overcome some difficulties, but overall they took upon themselves the responsibility of leading the changes. They had the full support of the business director responsible for all operations, but they also knew that it was their role to drive the organization forward, to challenge the assumptions that were common within the company, and to deliver results. The choice made, the decisions that followed, the issues related to possible conflicts were all taken, and dealt with successfully, in their stride.

DRAWING CONCLUSIONS FROM THE CASE STUDIES

It is always fraught with difficulties to draw conclusions from what appears to be a small sample. I have only used five organizations as part of the case studies used within this book, but what I have found here I have also found in all manner of organizations throughout the United Kingdom, Europe, Israel, North America, Australia, and New Zealand. In all cases, there is the same desire from the people at the top to succeed: all keen to secure the future of their organization, to see it perform into the future, providing jobs and wealth to the local community. The problem is that for many of those organizations the people at the top had lost the desire they started with, had stopped leading, and were simply managing. Many had simply given up, tired of the struggle of fighting against dominant paradigms such as local optima or a lack of leadership, and indeed ownership. It was in meeting these people that I started to develop what I now call the coaching quadrant—a simple construct to help me think about the best place to start to answer the questions I raised at the end of Chapter 7.

THE COACHING QUADRANT

In almost all of the many companies I have worked with over the years, I found the need to both challenge and often change what was going on, not just at the operational level but also at the level of relationships. The people I was working with were all in a different starting place—not that dissimilar but enough to require a different starting point. I needed to think about just what was needed at the start, what sort of help was being asked for, why did they think I might be able to help them. What I needed was an entry point like walking in through the front door of a large house and then being faced with more doors to choose from, based on my understanding of where the organization was, while standing in the hallway. So with all these questions in mind I examined what I had done in the past when faced with this dilemma and recognized that I could bracket the starting place into four distinct doorways. This in turn led to the creation of the coaching quadrant, or quad.

In almost all cases, what was about to happen within the organization involved change and, more often than not, one marked by a paradigm shift. This is the field of what is called "breakthrough solutions." In almost all cases where such a solution is required, there is an equal and pressing demand for a shift of paradigm. This often creates for many people tasked with leading such a change real difficulties in carrying out the actions required to implement the change. This is precisely the area of relationships. It is precisely the point where the leader needs to address the potential problem of what we call "leadership vacuum." The issue here is to help those stuck in the old paradigm break free, to achieve what they have never achieved before by doing things they have never countenanced before—this is the mark of true leadership to my mind. But the demands of the changes present a challenge to the relationships that have been formed within the organization and beyond. Now from the operational perspective it is vital to keep the changes moving forward, but is the plan robust? Have we taken account of the reservations of the team? Have we developed a full, robust, logical, do-able implementation plan, using a prerequisite tree and CCPM to implement the plan? And once this is all done, then do it again! The use of the flight crews within the context of the coaching cycle is critical, but it is for when an individual is experiencing problems in terms of relationships, perhaps one of the flight crew leaders, or flight crew members, or one of the top team within the organization that the coaching quad was developed. It consists of four key aspects, which I consider to be central to any coaching process, these being Healing, Reconciling, Sustaining, and Guiding. This is shown in Figure 8.2.

I have been working on these four aspects over many years, and they form the foundation of the work we have done in that time, but the pulling together of these aspects into one coherent piece is, to my mind, new. There is no fixed starting point; it is as if I have just walked through that front door mentioned earlier and am now faced with four more doors. Therefore the starting point for any coaching assignment can be anywhere within the "Quad," and the determination of the place to start is critical

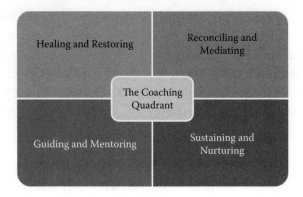

FIGURE 8.2
The coaching quadrant.

right at the beginning, hence the importance of listening before offering any advice. Think of it as a visit to the doctor, when before any treatment can begin there is a process of assessment and analysis to determine the problem; the same applies in coaching. Working out the answer to the question "where do I start?" is the most important choice I am going to make. Making the right choice here determines the success of the whole of the coaching process, and the decisions that follow and the issues I may meet are all determined by the choice of the starting place. So what do these doors look like?

Healing and Restoring

This might seem an odd title for this aspect, but many of our coaching projects in the past have centered on the need to restore broken relationships, between individuals and between teams, and even between departments or divisions! Clearly if relationships are broken to this extent then the first step is to seek out a map that restores these relationships and move to a situation where win-win is the dominant outcome of all negotiations and engagements throughout the organization. This is also about addressing the issues that are causing discomfort for people within the organization, the team, or sometimes within themselves. Change itself can cause trauma, and once more we find ourselves helping people cope with the demands that change can create. The use of the core TOC/TP tools such as clouds is of great value here; whether it be working on a one-to-one basis, which is often where I start, or working up to small groups, the cloud allows for the surfacing of assumptions and paradigms that may well be the cause of the issues being experienced. The use of other TOC/TP tools such as PRT to surface obstacles and develop intermediate objectives, or the Strategy and Tactics approach also work extremely well here. This is all about creating an environment where healing can take place, where past hurts and pain can be surfaced and addressed, "lancing the boil" as I often put it, such that what was once broken is mended.

Reconciling and Mediating

This aspect is very much where we set out to address the conflicts and issues that cause all manner of disputes. These conflicts can be between people, between functions, and sometimes the conflict of subordinating to the changes being asked of the individual. Of course there is overlap with other aspects of the Quad, but dealing with conflicts is a major aspect of our work, reconciling differences, and helping to create a win-win solution that restores a healthy balance within the organization and/or the team. If the subject matter here is a set of conflicts then once more the cloud offers a way forward, and again by working one-to-one and then in small groups it is possible to address what to some are insurmountable obstacles to any form of reconciliation and through very careful steps restore broken relationships and develop a new environment of win-win. This is not a simple task; it requires high levels of patience and will take time—but it can be done.

Sustaining and Nurturing

This aspect is all about trying to help with the question "what happens next?" For many people, the changes that take place are fully agreed, and any issues that arise as a result of the changes are overcome—but then there is this sense of "so what now?" The ability to sustain progress toward the goal is fundamental to any coaching activity. I have used this in both rugby and sailing where even the best know that there is a need to maintain the current level of expertise and excellence, and then to move to the next level. This applies to Olympic sailors and international rugby players as much as to any person working in any organization! This is all about the journey, a walking alongside someone, perhaps even the team, to enable them to maintain progress for themselves. I have put in place training programs that people inside the organization can take ownership of, develop, and thus maintain progress toward the goal. We have encouraged the creation and support for internal mentors and coaches who can assist people with problems and issues, using the same tools as myself plus others that they may already have, which leads us to the next aspect.

Guiding and Mentoring

This aspect is concerned with helping people recognize the direction they are taking today and checking as to whether this is the right direction! Many times we find people are working hard, but when you ask them about the goal they are striving to achieve, it becomes clear that they are working hard in the wrong direction! They might even be putting in more and more hours in order to drive themselves in precisely the wrong direction, and perhaps also driving their team in the same manner. Guiding starts with discovering the goal, and the necessary conditions that must be achieved for the goal to be achieved. Then, through a simple approach, we set out to determine if the current direction is the correct one. This is part of being able to paint a compelling picture of what the future might, or should, look like. This is where we ask, and try to help each person to answer, the questions "what" and "why." But then there are more steps to be taken, how to develop the journey, dealing with whatever is holding people back, the use of the compelling picture to encourage the involvement of more people, but at the same time knowing what the anchors are to keep us stable in the storms of life.

A REFLECTION ON LEADERSHIP

Gibbs (2005) observes that, when considering the world of leadership today, "Most of the leaders who have made it to the top of hierarchical institutions arrived there after years of faithful service" (p. 7). In that time, they gained insights, experience, skills, and not a few scars. However, as they emerge at the top they discover that the environment in which they must now operate is significantly different from that which has gone before. The world they thought they knew has changed, moved on, and often this new world is incomprehensible to them. They cannot comprehend, cannot grasp the new order. More today of what was done in the past is not going to be of any help in the future, or in any way effective. I remember an early lecture in my army career when it was stated that in almost every war the British Army has fought, the generals who were in command at the start were not around within a short period of time and certainly not by the end, replaced by those for whom the old ways of fighting were anathema and who embraced the new paradigms of warfare. I can only recommend *Who Moved My Cheese?* by Spencer Johnson (1998) for those wanting to know more about this aspect.

It is part and parcel of leadership to be able to develop self-discipline. Those that I have worked with have always been able to make sure they can master the following aspects:

1. Developing the ability to listen
2. Committing to the long haul
3. Making time for reflection to refocus and renew strength
4. Looking inside for the "problem" before looking outside

Leaders, as described by Gibbs (2005), must be trained to "observe and interpret the cultural changes taking place in society" (p. 49). Another to highlight this is Andy Grove (1995), a former CEO of Intel Corporation, with his use of the term "strategic inflexion point." One of the key changes affecting those trying to lead organizations today is a fundamental shift in communications—primarily through the use of smartphones and social media, such as Twitter and Facebook. This is having an impact on the structures in use. There is a clear shift taking place from hierarchical structures to networked structures. The paradigm of the hierarchy and all that it contains is being challenged, and in some cases dispensed with, in favor of a network paradigm (see Gibbs, 2005, Chapter 4, for more on this aspect). Today, as Gibbs argues, "leadership is about connecting not controlling" (p. 93), and this aspect is only going to grow ever more dominant in the years to come. For Gibbs, this means that as leaders, "we must be prepared to re-examine our assumptions in the light of continually changing circumstances" (p. 98).

The process of defining the broad picture is central to the leader. Identifying the mission—the goal of the organization—incubating that mission into a vision for people to take hold of and feel that they can not only make a contribution to, but also own that vision, lies at the start. For the leader, it is important to see the current state as a provisional reality, one that they, with the rest of the team, are going to change, taking all toward a future that is a consequence of the hope lying within the goal. Once this has been started, turning that vision, the mission, into something everyone can be passionate about is the next step. Leaders inspire passion, not for a continuance of the present but for the achievement of the future. This is where painting the compelling picture coupled with widespread ownership of the future hope has such an impact. Of course, this is also where the flight crew helps to reinforce the picture. What follows is the translation of the vision, the mission, into a strategic plan, a course of action that turns vision into reality and releases the team's imagination and the natural creativity that lies within most people in such a way that the team itself is inspired to achieve more than they could ever imagine; this is then cascaded down through the whole of the organization.

FINAL THOUGHTS

This has been a frustrating journey at times. Working with a range of clients over the past six or seven years has shown me that many organizations around the globe face real problems, real pressures, that create unique choices. I have met people desperate to make a difference to their organizations, desperate to make better choices than those already made in the past, but the question that dominated this quest was simply this— how to make a sound choice? Even starting the journey of leading an organization is a choice. Some accept the choice, some seek the choice, some try to avoid it, and others simply have it thrust upon them; but in all cases, once the person has taken up the reins, they need to make choices, and the way in which they do so, the level of rigor they apply before making that choice pays all manner of dividends in the future.

To see so many people frustrated by their inability to lead, by the lack of opportunity to lead, fearful of showing an inclination to lead, was disheartening. Yet at the same time I met those who simply did not accept the status quo, refused to conform to a paradigm that they knew intuitively was wrong, and set out to change things. Often they did so at some considerable threat to their well-being, but that did not put them off—it simply stoked the fire within to strive ever more to arrive at where they knew they had to be, and where their team and organization needed to be.

In this book, I have tried to paint a picture of what life is like in many companies today, the highs and lows. I am always in awe of those who try to make the changes they know are needed. They have a stamina and bravery I can only imagine. Over the years, I have used many tools and techniques drawn from many years of study and application. There are so many more, but that is not the issue. For those who wish to lead, they seek out the tools they require and do not stop looking until they find them. They also seek out the people they need to make the whole thing happen, for they know they cannot do it alone, whatever "it" might be. I have sat in their offices, walked around their organizations with them, watched how they interact with people, treating them with respect, asking them for their opinion, never afraid of being questioned, confident in their ability to listen, and to think and to lead. It is to them that I offer my congratulations for what they achieve in the hearts and minds of those around them. Leaders without scars have never led; leaders who have never failed have never led. This book is dedicated to those I have met and listened to. They have told me about the lessons they have learned, the scars received, the mistakes made, and yet what comes across most clearly and most inspires my admiration is the indomitable spirit that all leaders have and which leads you to follow them and their example.

REFERENCES AND FURTHER READING

Gamble, R. *Jesus the Evangelist*. Eastbourne, UK: David C. Cook, 2009.

Gibbs, E. *Leadership Next—Changing Leaders in a Changing Culture*. Nottingham, UK: Inter-Varsity Press, 2005.

Grove, A. *Only the Paranoid Survive*. New York: Doubleday, 1995.

Johnson, S. *Who Moved My Cheese*? New York: Putnam, 1998.

Katzenbach, J. R. *Real Change Leaders*. New York: Times Business, 1995.

Index

About the Author

Ted Hutchin, PhD, is the managing director of I & J Munn and principal of the TOC-Lean Institute. He is also a fellow of the Chartered Management Institute, a member of the Chartered Institute of Personnel & Development, and an industrial fellow in the University of Nottingham Business School.

In his work with TOC he has led the teaching, implementation, and ongoing coaching support across the full range of TOC applications throughout the manufacturing industry and also into the service and voluntary sectors with organizations as diverse as hospitals and the Anglican Church. He has lectured on the Masters in Supply Chain Management and the MBA within the Business School at the University of Nottingham and also on similar subjects at Cranfield University.

As can be seen from his research and writing over the past twenty-five years, the dominant theme has been the management of change and the problems and issues change creates for people. He has a proven ability to guide people in the creation of breakthrough solutions that get to grip with the core issues of the organization, the team, and the person's own life. Using a holistic approach to addressing such issues and developing robust solutions that move people forward toward their goals in life is central to the work he does today.

During many implementations of TOC he has met and worked with people who have asked for help in addressing their own individual problems and issues in achieving their life goals. This inspired him to develop the Personal Coaching program where time is spent on a one-to-one basis, addressing those core issues that seem to stand in the way of personal goals and developing breakthrough solutions that overcome whatever the blockage might be. It is this aspect of his professional work that led to the writing of this book.

PERSONAL INTERESTS

Outside of his professional life, he is a lay reader and evangelist with the Diocese of Leicester. He enjoys classic car rallies in his 1968 MGC GT with his wife and has been a keen sailor in the Laser class, having taken part in various championships from National through European to World Masters, including the Laser World Masters in Melbourne in 1999. He has played rugby for Nottingham RFC, and enjoys playing blues and folk music and participating in local musical productions.